. . . an astonishing array of poems in varying styles and multiple themes. Bernard, co-editor of *Caveat Lector,* may be one of San Francisco's best kept lyric secrets. His depth of imagination and metaphysical range stands out among today's facile poetry rappers or LANGUAGE descendants. There are echoes of Yeats, Wallace Stevens, and Eliot among others, but in the end the poetry belongs to the unfashionably erudite Mr. Bernard.

—IVAN ARGÜELLES, AUTHOR OF *HOIL* and *Cien Sonetos*

By turns tender and sarcastically fierce, Christopher Bernard's book is the lyrical antidote for our media-ridden end days. . . . Bernard's supple language draws on tradition, including the song-like verses of Robert Louis Stevenson, to imagine "clouds of flaming butterflies, the coming century." But hopefulness arises, because in Bernard's vision it must, in a world where you can "scratch on the ice spring's forgotten name." With humor, grace, and human insight, Bernard leads us toward our ever-nearing future.

—KEITH EKISS, AUTHOR OF *Pima Road Notebook*
AND TRANSLATOR OF *The Fire's Journey,* by Eunice Odio

. . . a vibrant and focused collection. . . . Standing in an imperfect world, this poet knows that without words in the right places our humanity is very much in question.

—MARVIN R. HIEMSTRA, AUTHOR OF *Raven Knows:*
Your Smile is Unique

. . . finds Christopher Bernard at his best: furiously lashing out at injustices . . . yet often giving the reader glimpses of hope.

—MARY MACKEY, WINNER OF THE 2019 ERIC HOFFER SMALL PRESS AWARD
FOR *The Jaguars That Prowl Our Dreams*

The Socialist's Garden of Verses

THE

SOCIALIST'S

GARDEN

OF

VERSES

CHRISTOPHER BERNARD

A Caveat Lector Book

REGENT PRESS
Berkeley, California

[paperback]
ISBN 13: 978-1-58790-530-8
ISBN 10: 1-58790-530-2

[e-book]
ISBN 13: 978-1-58790-531-5
ISBN 10: 1-58790-531-0

Library of Congress Cataloging-in-Publication Data

Name: Bernard, Christopher, 1950- author.
Title: The socialist's garden of verses / Christopher Bernard.
Description: Berkeley, California : Regent Press, 2021. | "A *Caveat Lector*
  Book." | Summary: Identifiers: LCCN 2020045297 (print) | LCCN
  2020045298 (ebook) | ISBN 9781587905308 (trade paperback) | ISBN
  9781587905315 (Kindle edition)
Subjects: LCGFT: Poetry.
Classification: LCC PS3602.E7593 S66 2021 (print) | LCC PS3602.E7593
  (ebook) | DDC 811/.6–dc23
LC record available at https://lccn.loc.gov/2020045297
LC ebook record available at https://lccn.loc.gov/2020045298

Cover: "Colorful Architectonic" (detail), by Lyubov Popova

Manufactured in the U.S.A.

REGENT PRESS
Berkeley, California
www.regentpress.net

In memory of
Sidney Grolnic
and
Harry Overholtzer,
musicians, friends, life-long allies

Pessimism of the intellect, optimism of the will.

—Antonio Gramsci

Only the weak have any humanity. The strong are at each
other's throats.   —Attributed to Dr. Eugeniusz Łazowski

Contents

Prelude in Hell

What Have We to Lose?

Dispatches From Pandemia

Faust Closes the Books on the Modern Age

Señor Despair and the Angel

Miracle

Kind reader,

The bulk of this book was written during the years 2016 through 2019, after the shocking election of a president who does not need to be named here. In fact, the book was largely written under the deepening shadow of those years.

Now that the book is appearing, we are close to a new election where the fate of the nation hangs in the balance (I would ask to be excused for using so weathered a cliché, except that never was one more apt, more ominous, or more true) between our current president and a very promising rival.

The year 2020 is likely to leave a mark on many lives that will not soon be forgotten, and the year's alarms are moving toward a climax even as we go to press. Will the year end in more confusion and fear, roiling political and economic emergencies, storm and fire, desperation and disease that have engulfed much, in some cases all, of the country, or with signs of a healing after months of trauma, with something like hope, decency, good judgement, neighborly goodwill and responsible leadership, and a return to the good health so many of us have taken for granted, but we now realize is so fragile? To say nothing of considerably better luck.

One section of this book is called "What Have We to Lose?" Perhaps a more important question now is, What have we to win?

—*Christopher Bernard*
September 2020

Prelude in Hell

November 8, 2016

You saw the beginning of the end of the world tonight.
It spoke from the TV set like a mouth
eating the air between you and its face.
Nothingness, of course, cannot be;
yet there it lay,
insisting, in its eyeless simplicity,
at your feet the pit was not a grave
and death was not the vise around your heart.
No: it was a monument in the making.
And greatness would not be its final stage.
It seemed a dream condemning the land:
"Unleash the demon, and heaven will descend."
America and God and capital,
freedom and our greatness and the end
of a world that you do not understand.

The Genesis of T#$%!landia

In the beginning Donald remodeled the heavens and the earth. And the heavens were sublimely beautiful and the earth was a pleasing place, but Donald was without form and void, and he hovered like a wrathful cloud over the deep.

And Donald said, Let there be Darkness. And there was darkness.

And Donald saw the darkness, that it was bad, real bad, and Donald divided the darkness from the light.

And he called the darkness day and the light he called the night. And evening and midnight were the first day.

And Donald said let there be a really classy casino town on an island, like Atlantic City, but that doesn't go bankrupt this time, in the midst of the waters, and let it divide the waters from the waters, you know like a martini before you shake it.

And Donald made the really classy casino island town and divided the waters which were under the island from those which were above, where Donald of course would be living in the penthouse.

And he called the really classy casino island Heaven. And evening and midnight were the second day.

And Donald said, Let all of the waters that were under the

casino island be gathered together into one place: it will make Mar-a-Lago the coolest resort ever.

And Donald called the dry land T#$%/landia and the gathering together of the waters he called the Largest Swimming Pool in Florida.

And Donald said, Let the earth bring forth grass, herb, maryjane, whatever you want to call it, just as long as it keeps everybody relaxed, people are getting way too excited, and we don't want that: and it was so.

And the earth brought forth grass, herb, maryjane and whatever you call it, and everybody became very, very relaxed, unconscious even, like, comatose, so he could do whatever he wanted as long as he didn't tax it; and Donald saw that it was bad, real bad.

And evening and midnight were the third day.

And Donald said, Let there be lights in the casino island of heaven to confuse day and night, so those poor losers will never, ever know what time it is: and it was so.

And Donald made two great lights; a great emoji with orange hair to rule the day, and a grouchy emoji (though still with orange hair) to rule the night: he made the stars who are famous for absolutely nothing at all, also.

And Donald set them in the great casino island of heaven to give light that was pretty indistinguishable from dark-

17

ness, upon the earth, to rule over day and night and con-
fuse everybody, all the time, as to which was which, so that
they would never again know which way was up, or frankly
know their butts from a hole in the ground; and Donald saw
that it was bad, real bad.

And evening and midnight were the fourth day.

And Donald said, Let the waters bring forth abundantly mov-
ing creatures that have life, and birdies that may fly above
the earth in the casino island of heaven; they will really in-
crease the entertainment, believe me.

And Donald created great whale-like monster companies
that paid no taxes (because they were, technically, bank-
rupt), and smaller companies that made money by cheat-
ing the losers he had not gotten around to creating yet, and
every winged shyster and con man you can imagine: and
Donald saw that it was bad, real bad.

And Donald said, Be fruitful, and multiply, and fill the NAS-
DAQ and NYSE with numbers that threaten to grow into the
sky, and let foul companies multiply across the earth.

And evening and midnight were the fifth day.

And Donald said, Let the earth bring forth toxins and carbon
dioxide and methane: and it was so: and Donald saw that it
was bad; holy smokes, it was bad, but (as Donald says), hey
you can't make an omelette without breaking some eggs. If
nature doesn't like it, nature can shove it.

And Donald said, Let us make a guy in my image, after my
likeness—a smaller Donald who does all things like Me, says

all things like Me, who every day in every way reminds Me of Me, smart, rich, with an amazing temperament (except when I don't get what I want, then I destroy you with a killer quote that nobody will ever forget), and let him have dominion over the fish of the sea and the fowl of the air and the cattle and over all the earth and over all those creepy crawlers who creep even me out, except of course whatever is on My personal estate of Mar-a-Lago, whose dimensions are still being negotiated (though, I'm telling you, it'll be the hugest estate ever).

So Donald created man in his own image, in the image of Donald created he him; male and female created he them, because, let's face it guys, you can't grab a pussy unless there's a girl attached to it.

And Donald blessed them, and said unto them, Be fruitful, and multiply, and replenish the earth and subdue it (because if you don't, I will), and have dominion over the fish of the sea and the fowl of the air and over every living thing that moves across the earth (except for those items mentioned in re Mar-a-Lago).

And Donald saw everything that he had made, and, behold, it was bad, it was real bad; it was really, really bad. And the evening and midnight were the sixth day.

And on the seventh day, Donald rested. And he lay down in his spectacular penthouse on the island casino of heaven and slept (except to get up to watch the all-night cable news channels, which he was already beginning to regret creating, and tweet about stuff that really irritated him, which was almost all of it) in the profound darkness of his world.

Invocation

Fragment engraved in concrete on a sunken island off the
coast of Hoboken, called Manhattan; ca. 2016 CE

T#$%!tilleus' baneful wrath resound, O Goddess that imposed
Infinite sorrows upon that world, and many poor Dems loosed
From heads sclerotic, sent them far to that invisible cave
Where no poll comforts, the night's results to media vultures gave.
Sing, O Muse, of the battle that led to the wretchedness of Hillary,
Doyenne of the last hope of the Clintons [indecipherable]
……….. baleful ….. insult to the …. and lunacy [lunatic?] …
…………………… choose ……… or ………………...
…..… end of ev[erything? everyone? everywhere?]…………

T#$%! Chaucer

Whan Novembre with his shoures ne soote
The droghte of sumer hath perced to the roote,
And bathed every veyne in swich liquor
That wyne can nowe be pressed from every flour,
Whan Foxe News eek with its bitterr breeth
Depresséd hath in every holt and heeth
The lamentable Dems, and the ageing sonne
Hath in thee his last halve cours yronne,
And smale foweles maken threnodye,
That slepen al the nyght with open ye
Acause they cannot slepe, for comes this bro,
And all must ende that we will ever knowe,
Then voters con to go to polling places
To cast their votes yn the correct spaces.

And so they came this yeere and voted dead
The world that made them, and us buriéd.

The Love Song of Donald J. T#$%!

Let us go then, you and I,
When election night is spread out against the sky
Like a voter etherized upon a table.

Let us go, through certain Wisconsin, Michigan, and Pennsylvania
    streets,
The muttering retreats
Of one-night stands in a shiny T#$%! Hotel
And cheap restaurants with flip-top hamburger shells;
Streets, like CNN, that follow a tedious argument
Of insidious intent
To lead you to an overwhelming question. . . .
Oh, do not ask, "What is it?"
Let us grab a p***y and make our visit.

In the room the hotties come and go,
Talking of Rudie and Pompeo and Barr and every other bozo.

Indeed there will be time
To wonder, "Do I dare?" and "Do I dare?"
Time to turn and descend a certain tower's stair
With a bald spot in the middle of my orange hair
(They will say: "How his hair is getting thin!"),
My bespoke coat, my collar mounting firmly to my chin,
My neck tie never modest but certainly rich, asserted by a really
    fabulous pin.
(They will say: "But how his hands are small, and how his legs are
    thin!")

CHRISTOPHER BERNARD

Do I dare
Disturb the universe?

What is this that I see before me?
A voting machine?
What does it mean?
I always vote by mail!

In the room the hotties come and go,
Talking of Rudie and Pompeo and Barr and every other bozo.

We have lingered in the chambers of Mar-a-Lago by the sea
By sea-girls wreathed with seaweed red and brown—and I mean,
    very brown—
Till the voters' voices wake us, and we drown.

Mr. T#$%!ollinax

When Mr.T#%$/ollinax walked across the United States
His laughter fell like a bull's cock among the teacups.
I thought of W., now a shy figure in the manzanita,
And of H.W. in the shrubbery
Slobbering over the hot babe on the swing.
In the palace of Mrs. Flaccus at Professor Ernest Doolittle's
He laughed like a psychotic poodle.
His laughter was quite subversive, though renowned,
Like the old man's demented tittering
Hidden under the dying coral reefs.
I looked for the head of Mr.T#%$/ollinax rolling under his limo,
Or grinning on a screen
Of a topless bar in Dubuque or Sioux Falls,
With tar sand in its hair.
I heard the beat of a satyr's goat-like hooves over Manhattan
    cement
As his acrid insults devoured the afternoon.
"He is a charming man, when you get to know him." "But after all
    what did he mean?"
"His pointed ears, his half-eaten eyes . . . he must be unbalanced."
"There was something he said I might have challenged—
A thousand things, but now—"
Of the dowager Mrs. Flaccus and Professor and Mrs. Doolittle
I remember only this: a piece of toast.
And of Mr.T#%$/ollinax his smiling, munching teeth.

T#$%! Among the Nightingales

Donald Trump spreads his knees
Letting his hair hang down to laugh.
I can't believe it! That was too easy.
Now I've got to perform, not half.

The circles of the stormy moon
Slide south from Fifth Avenue toward the Potomac.
Death and Sarah Palin roam
Like Monitor circling the Merrimac.

Giddy Newt and Mitch McConnell
Chortle, and Paul Ryan smiles,
The Tea Party prepares for a taste of Donald,
Nancy dances with democratic guile.

The host with someone indistinct
Converses at the door apart.
The voters who elected Trump
Are singing of the Sacred Heart:

They sang within the bloody wood
Where the old Founders beat their slaves
And kept their women properly
And burnt to dead gods in black caves.

T#$%! Emily

The Donald selects his own society,
Then slams the door.
His divine majority
The mobs adore:

Unmoved he notes diplomats pausing
At his locked gate.
Unmoved, a journalist kneeling
On his doormat.

I've known him from a nation
Choose (if she's hot) one,
Then clench the hose of his attention
Like bone.

Basho T#$%! ʲ

You call this a *what?*
It doesn't even. Look, believe me:
My poems. They *rhyme.*

The Waste T#$%!

November is the cruellest month, breeding
Electoral victories out of the dead land, mixing
Xenophobes and white Christians, stirring
Dull brains—and I mean dull! Sad!—with autumn rain.
Spring kept us busy, covering
The world with incredulous laughter, feeding
The media with bitter tubers they took like drugs.
Summer surprised us, coming over the Jackson gases
With more than Philadelphian love: it was fabulous!

What are the roots that clutch, which branches grow
Out of this stony rubbish? Ech, I won!
And now I gotta rule? Boy, this was so not supposed to happen.

Madame Sosostris, famous clairvoyante,
Is known to be the wisest woman in Queens.
Though you could have fooled me. Here, said she,
Is your card, the Tower
(A really big mother—man, it's huge).
Here is Megan Kelly, the Lady of Fox,
The lady of situations.
Here is the Magician (he still looks like a Kenyan to me), here
    is the Wheel,
And here is the one-eyed merchant—wait, that can't be right, it
    looks like me.
I don't find the Hanged Man, with the Republican

Bow-tie over the neoliberal tree.
I see crowds of people marching down Fifth Avenue.
Thank you, thank you. I know you hate me, but, hey,
At least you keep calling out my name.
I'm bringing the horoscope myself, by the way.
Me, I've always been my own fortune teller.

O O O O that shake'em-up, Twitter-feed rag!
It's so inelegant,
So unintelligent.
"What shall I do now? What shall I do?"
I don't know—call Elizabeth Warren?
"I shall rush out as I am, and walk the street
With my hair down, so. [You've gotta be kidding me!]
     What shall we do tomorrow?
What shall we ever do?"

HURRY UP PLEASE IT'S TIME

Well, you could have voted.
To get rid of this Unreal City.
Washington is falling down falling down falling down.
Donald's mad againe.
Data sucks. Dayadvham Brennan. Damdata.
        Shame ye   shame ye   shame ye

President T#$%!'s First State of the Union Address

Madam Speaker, Mr. President, Members of Congress, and My Fellow Americans:

It is my pleasure and privilege to state here tonight—to everyone in this great chamber and to everyone across our country and around the world—that the Con of our Statedom is strong.

(Cheers, standing ovation.)

Never before have so many of my fellow Americans been so united as they are in their hopes for our great country. Never before have they been more ready to defend our nation's ideals, never before have they been more optimistic or more hopeful for the future. Never before have they been so bound to a single purpose.

(Cheers.)

I—and only I—have been able to bring together all of the disparate strains of our great nation into a single bond of amity, loyalty and hope.

Only I have ensured our strength abroad and our prosperity at home, our good name among the nations of the world and our strength of purpose in all that we do and will do for ourselves, our families and our posterity.

And I have done so by becoming the only thing that you pussies think about, dream about, fear, hate, loathe, email,

Christopher Bernard

post, tweet, Instagram, Tinder, TikTok, and have mass hysterical breakdowns every day all over the internet, television, radio and newspapers of our great land—I have become what only I could have done: *I* am the Con of the Statedom.

YOU have ME to thank for making America Great Again.

(Cheers, standing ovation.)

Because, believe me, before you guys made me president because of that crap document the Constitution (remember the Electoral College? Whoever came up with that lousy idea, I'll make him my next Attorney General—hear that, Jeff?) before that bullshit election that I didn't even want to WIN, people! this shithole country was the world's biggest loser anybody has ever seen since, like, the decline and fall of the Roman Empire—ever hear of that? This country was so over, it was like a Mexican rapist in the Bronx or Fat Roseanne having a cat fight with Crooked Hillary. SAD! You people were so screwed, all I had to do was show my you-know-what, and you all came running, RUNNING! Little America! Who needs to grab whatever when you guys couldn't stop sticking it in my face—I mean, come on!

And what happened? Now you can't shut up about it! You are getting so bonged, and there's nothing you can do about it for another three years. Count the days! Go ahead! I can wait.

31

Guess what, losers? YOU owe ME your whole messed up country. The New York Times would be filing for bankruptcy by now if it weren't for me!

And then you're talking about voting for—the Fat Lady Who Owns Weight Watchers? You gotta be kidding me! But guess what? They're won't be any more White House, they're won't be any more West Wing (eat your heart out, Charlie Sheen!), or Foggy Bottom (roll over, Rex!), there won't be any more Department of This or Department of That—hey, I'm sending all of them to Macy's, and we know where they're headed! The Fat Lady won't have a pot to piss in once I'm through with Washington. I'm going to drain the swamp, and then I'm going to stick it down the toilet. And then ride the escalator back up Trump Tower back in New York, where they love me, and they'll love me even more, because I will have done what not a single Democrat has been able to do in the last two hundred years.

I say: Let the country BIDE 'N' BERN with Camel Face, Pocahontas and the Squad, people! Because I—and only I— have Made America Safe for Socialism.

I hope all you losers have a totally lousy life. And May God Bless America—because, believe me, this covfefe* could only have happened here—bigly!

(Cheers, standing ovation for the next 1,084 days.)

---

*Note this stunning example of our commander-in-chief's unparalleled foresight in predicting the novel coronavirus hoax—"Covid-19"!—of 2020.

See the literary subtlety of the allusion: "cov" (for "covid") plus "fefe" for "fake news-heh-heh!" A stunning example of his unique "stable genius" at work in an extemporaneous inspiration of the moment.

What Have We To Lose?

Between Two Cups of Time

During the late nineteenth century, when I was young,
crinoline and albatross took wing,
a captain's pipe cracked jokes with a frock coat,
and pince-nez paraded proudly in his yellow waistcoat.
Schooners warmed politely to locomotives,
Wellingtons grew rubbers in a tub,
bustles bustled, a whalebone muslin fling
waltzed between two parasols, two hats,
and twenty garrisoned shakos, a palette, and a warm cravatte.

I would walk down dreaming boulevards,
a dancer in my stunned and frail bouquet,
my mouth a half-dead tea rose, all my eyes
staring over whitened canvas seas
at clouds of flaming butterflies, the coming century.

The Night of February

God Storm he take the house in hand
and shake like a cup of dice.
He curse, he whisper, all night,
like a drunken cadet in an all-night casino,
whisper sweet nothings to the bones,
shout threats, he intone promises.
What come up? Live—or die?
Double eight, or snake eyes?

He blow on his fist—hear the howling wind!—
for luck . . .

When day dawn,
his eyes still weeping.

My Python

I keep a python in my throat.
Since childhood, it sleeps in the sun of my health,
its yellow eyes open in the winter cold
when, to stay alive, it must flex its mastery.
I think it a python for it kills by strangulation,
and once each year, for as long as I remember,
it tries to strangle me.
We writhe in battle, my hands on its neck,
its coils around my air.

Tonight it brought me the one true fear:
for a minute that lasted long as a nightmare,
I woke, my throat seized in its dry, cold skin.
I shouted, but no shout came;
my voice was small as a yell across a canyon;
when it reached me, it pressed against my ear
a mocking wheeze.
I watched my breathing turn to stone,
a page of ripped tin
aimlessly swinging. Throwing myself from bed,
I rushed about the apartment, demented with terror.

Yet I beat him down
in the end, this time,
though I did not kill him.
His grip dropped away,
and he slowly curled back into my lungs' shadows.
I can hear him among the confetti

of my most ancient childhood memories;
his scales are flecked with petals.
He vanishes for a season,
his tongue flickering in a hole in the pack ice,
as he waits patiently for our next embrace.

If he ever kills me, it will be like being killed by my childhood.

Opera Zedd

In the morning I walked past the opera.
The sundresses were waving like banners
and the boys did what boys usually do.
The ballroom was painted in pastels. Henry Moore
reclined in cheerful bronze under the enamel sky.
They were making dazzling arcs on the high trapeze.
Frankly I was having a hard time breathing,
it was so unutterably amazing.
Unutterably? Well, maybe scratch that.
The moon was still unseen,
though they told me it was harvest.
And the girls in pigtails were dancing. But their eyes
were hard. The blue angels
roared in the basement
like trapped tigers.

The Silk Road Caravan
Passes in the Night

What do I hear there, through the falling of the snow?
It is the sound of my lady dancing,
to her little silver bells.

What do I see, like ice on a country road?
It is the eyes of my lady dancing
to the glittering beating of the drums.

What do I feel when winter's scattering wind comes?
It is the beating of my heart dancing
to the lady and the bells and the ice and the snow and the
    road and the wind and the drums.

Primavera

The afternoon lies across the air
like a page of ice;
dazzling and shadowless.

You walk across it,
through it, beneath it,
looking for a crack in the light,
trying, without success, to hide.

The eyes you meet are gray as ashes.
The words you hear disappear like clouds.
A scarf lies abandoned on a curb.

Somewhere there is the sea,
a party's laughter, and someone is singing,
and summer holds the night in its arms.

"Behind the fog . . . "

Behind the fog Narcissus sleeps
next to cold Endymion.

Cold Dawn

The black concedes to gray—
a kind of wimpish black,
you might have said—a bruise
from an overnight drunk,
now hungover, staring blank—

or an attack
of migraine, salmonella
from eating dark that's gone bad—

turning its face from the day.

Of course,
it does not stop
there.

There
is a kind of frost-pane look
above the bank of towers
flanking downtown's edge,
it
melts, and a raw, damp breeze
sucks toward the west:

a face,
red ... then green ... then gold,
moves up the eastward pass
like a cartoon,

like a wound—
like a scar—
like a god—
like a conscience,
distantly smiling;

then,
in the county wards of space,
among a rush of irritable stars
like overworked nurses or bedbugs on fire,

a blot appears
of wild brilliance,
silent,
shouting,
announcing, with chanting tribes of angels,

quite terrible, quite
magnificent,
the dazzling wings of Quetzalcoatl
and the flaming, stampeding horses of the sun.

My Father's Rake

A neighbor borrowed a rake from my dad.
His own had broken off at the head,
and he needed to rake his vegetable patch:
the rocks were strangling his cabbages.
Dad lent his tools only with reluctance:
they were heirlooms going back to before the Great War;
in fact, he had borrowed his rake from his own dad,
but had forgotten to give it back, or something like that.
But the neighbor was persuasive: he'd return it in a week.
It was early summer. The hot months passed
and stole into the oak yellow reds and the rains
of the eastern fall. The cabbage patch
had long been harvested, and the ground was flat
with mud once again, and late random weeds
it was pointless to pull: winter would soon come.
But no rake: the neighbor hadn't given my dad back his tool,
so my dad—a patient, bookish, forgiving man—
knocked on his door. "Oh, that!" said the neighbor.
"I lent it to Bob." So my dad went to Bob.
"What rake? Oh, that rake! Hm . . . let me see now . . .
Yes! I gave it to Lawrence, who needed it to turn over
his potatoes." Of course, Lawrence had lent it too, to Al,
who'd lent it to Sam, who lent it to Paul,
who had been meaning to return it to Sam but forgot
where he'd left it—in his flowerbeds?
Or—no—in his vines?
Yes! The concord grapes! It must be there! "Fine!"
said my dad. Of course, it wasn't there either. With a sigh,

my dad came home. It might turn up in the spring,
the handle rotted through, the head and teeth rusted
from exposure, ugly and useless as it corroded back to earth,
    water and air.
My dad shrugged it off as just one more example
of the lesson he'd never learned (he told me many years later):
like that rake, though you keep it for so long it seems yours,
it isn't: you only borrow your life.
You can even lend it out, but don't be surprised if you
    never see it again,
because the truth is, you never really owned it.
The world is a dance without end between hope
and memory to the constantly changing music,
the grave, dissolving harmonies of reality;
nothing is lost or gained forever.
Everything we possess, everything we are—
body and mind and soul and spirit—
is held between the past and the present and the future
with outstretched hands forever.

A Child on Calvary

A young man hung on a cedar cross
to mind and heart held hope and grace,
sick healed, taught love, to wounds gave balm.
No greater insult hued with wrong
offended the eyes of the rich and strong.

This Messiah king must be rubbed out,
this Nazarene who dared their lie,
in a world where fear was the only force
men must honor: "Others must fear
as we fear—must, above all, fear us.
Let kindness despise its own still face.

"The Son of God! The Son of Man!
A mountebank, a charlatan!
A nobody no one will recall
a week from now." They give the cross a glance,
then make their plans for the evening dance.

The young man calls out;
his words sheathe a warning inside a shout:
"Father, forgive them for they know not what ..."
And yet they did. By evening dead,
the man is dropped from the crooked tree
and buried ... but we know the rest.
They say he rose.... Believe that still?
Or that he stays quite dead, well,
and sits not at his Father's right hand?

49

Or is there no heaven, and no hell?
And does he neither hate nor love
more than does a murdered dove?
Nor judge nor rule, command or mean,
a nagging, unexpungible meme,
a bit of the bad conscience of man?
The echo of an inscrutable demand
from the void we seed with gods' minds:
the law to love and live and die
without recriminating the divine?
A ghost haunting the future's past
formed of air, and hope, and dust,
a word in a book more closed than read,
an act of tenderness, a name in a prayer,
a holy myth of a once good man?

The last he saw, before he died,
was a child with its mother at the foot of the cross,
staring up at him and crying,
not knowing for whom—just crying, crying.

Phantom Buildings

They stand like a fog of boxes down the avenues,
dead soldiers at the back of abandoned bars,
hollow, drained of souls as of their spirits,
phantoms of the city, edifices quite wiped out
by cement sealed, through steel, to masks of glass.

The city that is is haunted by the city that was,
pedestals deprived of beauties as of gods,
towers of cloud that do not seem quite real.

They say if you squint you can see through the ghost buildings,
spectral, hard, crystal, concrete, dead,
and, out of the phantoms, the Real City appears.

Warms like the Sun

sealight through the open windows

tailfins chrome bumpers an antenna like a flagpost

a wool scarf smeared with snowflakes

raggedy towel and last year's bathing suit
the deliberate smell of mothballs
wet sand all over your feet
and what's that squeaky linoleum?

the screen door bangs open

little sister piping up, as usual:
hey man, *it's so cold*

warms like the sun

CHRISTOPHER BERNARD

Coffee with the Prophet

The café was bleakly funky,
once inside from the cold foggy streets,
unpainted at least since the '60s,
with, near the entrance, a papier-maché
witch head, a giddy dance of wire
propped on a nail, a poster above a juke box
from Barbarella, and a roach clip glued
to a fragment of vinyl from Verve
mounted on green velvet in the men's.
The Prophet sat in a corner
at the back, his hands folded over an ashtray
(they still allowed smoking in such places),
his eyelids heavy as stones.
I approached him in a wide, low spiral,
slow and careful. "Nieblas!"
he said. "You are too careful a hunter!
I hear your steps cracking the chaparral."
Surprised, I stopped. "Excuse me!"
I said, "Don Rafael! I didn't mean to ..." "Kill me?"
he said, his eyes staring toward the bar. "Well?"
I laughed nervously. "I am almost dead!" He grabbed me
by the hand (could he, as everyone said, really see?)
and pulled me down to a chair beside him.
"Nieblas," he said (my name is not Nieblas!)
"Long for you have I waited—a lifetime!
My gray hairs had almost given up hoping
your fingers would comb through them sweetly.
The darkness I live in has been the only comfort,

53

as it hid, always, your absence from me.
Nieblas!" He held my hand tighter.
"I have something to tell you. Hear closely."
He pulled my face down and his mouth breathed in
my ear, and I froze in a pure reflex,
part fear and part disgust. "My Nieblas,
I am the wind that will blow you away
to the end of the air and the sea.
Do not try to run, for I have you.
You will regret you did not kill me."
"My name is not Nieblas!" I shouted
"My name is not Nieblas!" I pulled away
and ran out of the café in a panic
and ran down the foggy street, shouting to everyone
I passed till the fog swallowed me.

I now live in a forest away from the city
and hide when I hear humans come. My hair
is gray now as the Prophet's. I hear,
when the fog ascends from the valleys
in the spring, a bird seems to call from the trees,
"Nieblas! Nieblas!" and I know that it means me.

Romantic Group in a
Prospect of Mountains

It displays a nameless mountainscape
powdered thick with snow—
the striations across their faces, like a slice of thousand-layer cake,
showing the rock once lay
for many millions of years at the bottom of the sea.
The photo covers the wall of a basement café.

Deep in the still lake at their feet the mountains' reflections hang.
And on the radio, the "Moonlight"
sonata, in an arrangement
for oboe, piano, strings begins
its slightly saccharine round.

A curiously—almost ludicrously—romantic image, this.
Obermann, Byron, Shelley
glare amiably around them in some Swiss album of time.
Turner thrusts his easel firmly into a snowbank.
Stendhal peers from his window, alone, as he crosses the Simplon
    Pass.
In a wild valley, a woman dreams
of a monster seeking its creator as it wanders the arctic ice.
Beethoven listens to the silence
rising from his hands.

The Sleepwalker

A certain man there was
who often walked in his sleep.
He'd wake with mud on his feet
and aches in his hands.

One day he wakes to the rage
of a crowd mobbing the street
in front of his house and chanting
his name. It terrifies him.

Why do they hate me? he whispers.
In response they chant in a roar.
"Why do you hate me?" he screams.
They scream, "You! Murderer!"

On his dark walks in sleep
through the streets of the night,
he killed a man—killed ten;
then killed dozens more;
old, middle-aged, young.
Now the town has found him,
and wants its justice raw.

There are whole nations like this
assassin in the dark:
they sleep when they kill. They are shocked
when the world seeks revenge on them.

After Longley After Amergin

Who is that old child, brash
As a nameless avatar
Who is that heartbroken sombrero
And the noise of a cracked guitar
Who is that gray armadillo
That soaks in the rain of the run
Who is that Tasmanian devil
Wreaking revenge on Washington
Who is that bucket of cherries
Upon the jonquil stone
Who is that tilbury bridge
In the dreams of Chatterton
Who are those ashes of lace
That scatter through Lille over the snow
Who is that train of the ant
That knows no up or below
Who is that silence of sleeping
In the darkness of teacups and bread
Who is that dash on the window
And the whispering sheet on the bed
Who is not this and not that
And wanders the world like the wind
Who is a withering thread
And who is it no one will know

I am that old child, brash
As a nameless avatar
I am that heartbroken sombrero

And the noise of a cracked guitar
I am that gray armadillo
That soaks in the rain of the run
I am that Tasmanian devil
Wreaking revenge on Washington
I am that bucket of cherries
Upon the jonquil stone
I am that tilbury bridge
In the dreams of Chatterton
I am those ashes of lace
That scatter through Lille over the snow
I am that train of the ant
That knows no up or below
I am that silence of sleeping
In the darkness of teacups and bread
I am that dash on the window
And the whispering sheet on the bed
I am not this and not that
I wander the world like the wind
I am a withering thread
And who I am no one will know

Seascape, Summer 2010

granite northern sea
shredded leaves of green
and many voices
far out to a ragged horizon

come back to me as if
I had never left

a spritz of birds
roils over
the waves' shaggy roar

disperse from me as if
I had never been

Chardonnay

Sitting after dinner, breathing in a chardonnay,
and flirting idly with a faith, long betrayed,
from my deeply charmed childhood and my rebellious, lyrical
    youth,
I realized, with a shock to this bankrupt system of mine,
what I thought might be called, indeed, a small truth:
that fragrance, which seemed to me, to be candid, half divine
and rising, in blissful zeal, on its breath of fumé,
proved beyond a doubt an extraordinary thing
(not scientifically, but then science can't prove anything);
delighting in its notes of peach, lemon, orange peel,
its slight tannin edge, and its very slow decay:
that paradise—yes, paradise—I repeat: paradise is real.

It was a shocking thought. Though why? Hell is real,
purgatory a probability, life unsure, death certain,
oblivion likely, annihilation almost desirable, a curtain
between the anticipation and the hammer on the thumb,
a kind of relief anyway, to know what's to come
for sure. But joy? contentment? hope
that stands an actual chance?—No,
I told myself, and yet, yet—yes,
something like that prosaically named Thing: happiness,
a rooted love for the world that is,
in a way beyond prediction or expectation, like a kiss
returned when least hoped for (yet most needed),
on the shoulder a casual caress, a reed
fluting the dusk, less than a breath,

a wing's tip brushing the back of your neck, death
of a despair I have lived with since leaving the home
my childhood left me. To this I had come:
in nothing's embrace, there was something—no, someone—
without shape or name, furtive, rustling, half woman,
half child, as old as a cloud or the world,
a zephyr in a fluttering of shadow and sun,
the dancing of chance, as the chardonnay swirled,
and the air pulled me down, and I drowned in love.

Phantom Sun

Walking out of the city grunge
into an immense canvas by Turner:

        cerulean, lapis, crimson

      a whorl of turquoise and pinks
      like stains of grass and roses, a nautilus

       a freighter of coal smoke
          disintegrating

                 mauves
      angels' lips

     and a trace of crushed pine smoking into yellow,

      hung above a sea as gray as pewter,

       against, smudged with ivory,
       a profoundly incautious night
       scoured by—

not the cyclops of the darkness in the molten azure
of the lake of the cave of the sky—

     but a glaring splotch of perpetual fusion
     reaction roaring silently against the stars

and, like a hole in a mask,

a second,

a hooded mirage
in a heavy, slow blink of nimbo-cumulus
within the claw of tongues of the welkin's chaos.

An illusion.

Or God's eyes.

Brief Poems

a coyote walks insouciantly down Broadway

*

a young student stares at her laptop
the laptop stares back at the young student

the older student gently turns a page

*

strong wind
a hollow thump
a swift streaks through the darkness

*

crows against summer clouds

coffee stains on a tablecloth

*

her grandfather was an acrobat
his granddaughter walks across the deck on her hands

*

the gardener
apologizes
as he destroys the garden

the vines are gone
no one told them
about the hummingbirds

*

scattered clothing

lovers running laughing toward the sea

Body of the Goddess

The woods tangle her fingers,
her knees shadow the hills,
the valleys bare her secrets,
her eyes betray the sun;

the ocean is her dancing,
her anklets are the sand.
Her breasts are the clouds,
her sighs are the wind.

We play our games in her dark bed.
Listen: the sound of our laughing
is music to the ten thousand worlds.

Lo, we are her puppets—
our dramas in her arms,
tragedies, comedies, farces
over childish issues and causes—
her pets she pampers or releases
to the wild to see how we'll fare—
her peculiar invention: humanity,
that mirror that tells her beauty
and the truths she hews from the world.
Till she tires, and sweeps us away,
down the long ladder of childhood
and the spiral stairs of the dance,
back into being's toy chest
and the crucibles of matter and chance.

When we fare badly, she weeps for us,
for how can we know what we are?
Her weeping is rain and is snow.
She is kind: when our suffering is too much for us,
she wraps us in her arms and goes.

Travelers in the City of Saint Francis

In August it is the French,
in July the Germans,
on the streets of this sea-brushed compendium of earth's
    peoples.
In winter, from the antipodes,
the Australians ascend,
flanked by ageing New Zealanders
and the occasional defensive South African.

When a catastrophe at some other edge of the world
shouts from the news, soon emerges,
in the humiliating sun or half-glimpsed in street lights,
a stained skullcap, furtive hijab,
a slash of crimson on a yellow robe,
a wool sack lumpy with shattered hopes,
a baby in a shawl sleeping between distended shoulder blades,
cold eyes above burned mouths—
refugees from a world that knows no seasons for its disasters,
just noon and midnight.

Return

Across the darkness of the gulf,
the rose spins, majestic,
unfurling, expanding,
flower of destruction
scattering behind it petals from a fist of wind.

The ancient gods have returned.
They stalk the world in anger.
They grew in the heart of man.
Now they take their revenge.
"You placed yourself above us!
Now you are lower than the worm!
We are the mirrors of your pride!
The mirrors have shattered, you dance on the shattering."

A small voice rises on the wind:
"Take pity, gods, in your anger!
The wrong-doers you have not harmed:
the poor, weak, unprotected,
are crushed like worn pottery by your fury,
unjustly. Take pity!
Man's evil lies upon them:
do not add to their suffering!
Take pity, gods, on them!"

But the rains fall, unhearing,
the gods are deaf to the plea.
The water rises in destruction,
the petals of the rose of the seas.

The Divine Vessel Joins the Heavenly Palace

Today Shenzhou XI docks with Tiangong II
in the peace of the Dao
in the courtly whirlwind of the stars.
The Middle Kingdom dances thus with Heaven.
Heaven dances thus with the Middle Kingdom.
Who needs know more?
(Perhaps we need to know a good deal less!)

The universe we have sung into being:
perhaps we will learn to blow it out like a candle.
Our fingers on the bowl
leave their prints on the fragments.
The constellations dance to the music of our darkness.

Hawking

In falconry,
you raise your arm
on which the falcon's
talons hold,

remove the mask,
unleash the tie,
that hold him close,
and let him rise—

He spread his wings
like clouds, to rise,
brief empery
of sand and air,

repelled the land
to king the sky.
Where to fly,
the wind command,

into the wilderness
of this sky,
mortality
his hour deny?

We scan the air;
we wait.
          His eyes,
his eyes contain
all worlds, all skies.

71

"I Am a Squirrel"

She gnawed away at a little nut
in a most critterly way.
I turned to speak to my little sister,
but she blinked at me, and ran away.

I looked for her, up and down,
and high and low, and near and far.
Then recalled Dottie's
other little oddities:

the secret caches of acorns,
the piles of twigs, the hole in the oak
just so big
she could fit in, tight,

the old robe of mom's,
gray, long-furred, long,
wrapped round like a train
and worn like a stole,

the Davy Crockett hat
with the gray fox tail
adorning her chestnut head,
her furtive smile,

the nervous runs
she made over the grass,
her curious natterings,
the way she held her wrists.

And then I looked up:
she had climbed up a tree,
with the stole hanging, furrily,
and was looking down at me.

Her eyes were as blank
as a cat's. Her small hands
held the trunk like a squirrel,
then she vanished into the leaves.

Sometimes in the evening
I see a squirrel cross the lawn.
It stops and stares at me,
almost wistfully, then runs on.

Radu Lupu's Schubert

When I died, the angels whispered
in my watery ear
the singing of the naiads
in the labyrinth of air,

and the echoes of the fingers
of a young, old Viennese
in a slow sonata
died with me, soft as a rose.

Hear the dark piano,
it stands stark as a tomb
on the precipice of pain
in the sweetness of a tune.

He holds the fretful features
of the canny gods of old
and resumes the malice of him
who would crack the secret wild-

ing, of the scattering of silver,
of the hands of music, dumb
as the dead bird's wings in autumn.
What's he singing? Let them come.

Whisper Me

He smiled, painfully.
"Whisper your words to me,"
he said, "do not shout,
please, if you would please me.

"Don't try to outmaster
the café's heavy bombast,
the rants and raves of fashion,
the lusty thunder malice
wreaks in its private wars,
resentment's long-lunged bitterness,
or success's brazen horns.

Mute them with your quietness.
Wield your poise like a knife.
I am deaf to the lightning
as I am blind to the drums,

yet I can hear your breathing.
in this noisy bar.
I could read your lips
across a battlefield."

O Sweet Illusion

a broken piece of onyx
in the young boy's hand
molasses glass a knife of coffee

a white station wagon
parked on a Mexican road

a plain of cinders laid out like the frosting on a layer cake

piled boulders brontisaurian
stegasaurian
megasaurian

pyroclasts geodes boom boom boom

river of lava broken plowlike in soft stony rills
to a smooth lake of stone where a village once stood

a finger print on a petrified doorknob

leaning against the sky
the rough two-handled volcano pursed and silent
a peak like a pair of puckered lips spouting a plume
     that reads
"Excelsior!" echoes "excelsior excelsior excelsior"

"dear volcano!" she whispers
"what a gift!"

dark sea of glass
glittering to the horizon
the violence forgotten
the devastating loveliness

When the Music Died

That day, under his breath no one sang
as he sauntered, without a care, through the lovely weather.
No one hummed to herself as she weeded the garden
or stepped casually out of the house's darkness.
No unsteady piano tripped, knocking
at the neighbor's sleeping window.
The radio's static wiped a violin's
cheeks with a cold handkerchief.

A wedding held its breath under the brilliant chandeliers.
A funeral turned into white stone.
The churches listened, paralyzed, to the silence of the bells.

The children came down with an incurable illness.
Their voices vanished, their ears grew hungry as corn.
Many became cripples, unable to leave their beds. Some died.
Their parents were not even able to sing their mourning.

The glaciers advanced down the mountains toward the cities
even as the birds
sang their warnings in an ancient tongue
dead as Petra and Uxmal.

The blues band stared, puzzled, at their instruments:
what could such outlandish objects possibly be for?
The opera house folded up like a tent,
and the ballerinas disbanded like a demobilized army
and wandered the streets, homeless and beautiful.

At the Docks

Great white horses,
their heads raised, alert,
a hundred feet tall
high above the wharves,
listening to the wind,
their nostrils alert, trembling.

The Angry Goat of Carrickfergus

He glowered through the H&M window pane
After knocking down shoppers in the shop-and-go lane.
His horns shone with a preening disdain—
The indignant goat of Carrickfergus.

He ate all the flowers from the stall,
Then he trotted, irate, up and down the mall.
He'd had enough, nor was that all—
That furious goat of Carrickfergus.

People! Everywhere!—The gall!
Cement where pastures stood—tall
Oaks—cars gassing, to appall
A peaceful animal to asperge us!

"Up with this I shall not put!"
Muttered to himself the angry goat
As his beard wagged haughtily and he readied to butt
With all his strength, and a mighty curse.

He lowered his head and ground his hoof
As a truck passed under the entrance roof,
And prepared to charge to his final proof.
Which was the end of the angry goat of Carrickfergus.

On Being Uninteresting

Faded, uncool, with a taste for beige,
tobacco, bourbon, ketchup-red braces,
polka-dot bowties, white leather shoes, and Old Spice cologne,
with his spotless VHS collection of "Mary Hartmann! Mary
    Hartmann!"
and other esoterica of forgotten '70s TV,
with his ashtray (remember ashtrays?)
from Copacabana with a little cocktail parasol
in one of the indents where middle-aged VPs laid, in better times,
their scofflaw cigars,
and an ancient, predigital mixtape of Burt Bacharach
on the point of breaking on his ramshackle Walkman
set on Replay forever:
these mark the quaintly savage armor shielding him from our
interest in the hardened steel of a hipster's mockery.

He would call himself a fossil if it weren't an insult
to our unhappy ancestors who failed to make the grade;
all of us, eventually. Ah well. The kids know best
who merits wasting their time. He moves, quite unseen,
through crowds flocking the avenues, the lines before the Bobas,
the Taylor Swift lookalikes, the hackers in their sweats,
the ear-muffed soloists of downloaded apps
enscarfed in dithyrambs of Dr. Dred and The Everlasting Technique;
past swarms of wasps called Uber
in its grinning Nietzschean illusion
or Lyft, with its effervescent pink mustache and chromium snarl;
unnoticed or ignored as one more of the homeless

legions, nut case, possibly a molester
of the innocent, or a harmless nomad from the past
that the rest of us have eternally escaped:
a skull in a three-piece suit,
an exhortation, a warning.
"Stuck in the past." But not in the present.
Chooser of his own era. A dangerous man. Free.

The Children's Crusade

Black is the blood of the earth:
it burns when it meets the air.
The children lament in the twilight
at what their parents have done.

But their parents do not listen:
they watch the burning blood
and sing themselves to sleep
as they turn away from the sun.

The blood of the earth runs cold:
it burns to sweat and ice.
The parents dream with abandon.
The children, they have abandoned.

Beachdrift

clam shell curled like a calcium croissant
folds of shiny mylar: seaweed
long green whip with a little ball at the thick end
a crate in shreds sky bluer than an eye

stump of a freighter out of the horizon haze
a big ugly thing
covered with cars and pickled plums and carbonated sake
in stacks on its deck like teeth or the columns at Paestum

it looks like a big shoe
silent moonwalk over the ocean

it comes stealthily
grows huge
slips into the Golden Gate

the ocean is empty afterward
the ocean was empty before
the waves say adore adore adore

The Lady Said

Hypatia on a stony pier in the sun
as beautiful as a mind, its sensual fire,
traces a comet in the Egyptian sand
and lets the heavens fall into her hands.

What if earth is not the center
of the cosmos, but the great
star that seems to circle us,
the glorious sun? she whispers

in her mind, centuries before
the Polish stargazer guessed
how we wander lost in the maze
of the universal labyrinth.

But that man had learned to fear
the holy assassins haled in Rome:
he kept his secret till he must
suffer for everything he lost.

The ragged saints hear the lady
and smoke the ancient town with rage.
"We are the heart of the world's fear
spurned into a crust of love

burned into its opposite,
eternal fire beneath our feet!
Where men are born to sin and die:
the earth is the center of the universe,

no other where. The sun was made
to be our servant, not we its slave.
How dare this woman spite good sense!"
How dare any woman ...!" Just one kind.

"Harlot! Whore of Babylon!"
In rage they tore her from her book,
hurled her prideful mind to so much
Greek dust offending Egyptian mud.

Then took her by her marvelous hair
and stripped and stoned the beautiful body
and dragged it, shouting, through Alexandria's streets
beneath the sun.

With Them

The computer screen is crossed by a line
like a black thread. One or two tangles,
loops twisted and angled
like the shrunken remnant of a spider's web
or the map of a river.
Somewhere near the middle of the thread
are the boys. It is, so they tell us—
the correspondents, the speleologists,
the government officials, and engineers—
a small pocket of cavern,
between rock and water and air,
in the deep bowels of the mountain
where they await rescue before the coming monsoon.
The subterranean darkness
swims with islands of cell light,
illuminating the young faces like Halloween masks
from the chin, reversing the shadows to "really scare you."
The faces, far away as the reflections in an aquarium,
are childlike and smiling.

Haymaking

A big canvas.
Blank noon in a sultry field.
Flat yellow greens that ride up to an abruptly
cut off horizon.
A silence shrill with grasshoppers.
A young peasant dozes under his hat,
flat on his back in the grass.
The metal pail that held lunch
pewters, dull, in the weeds.

Next to him,
rumpled, slouched forward as if
she had just shot up,
half-startled asleep,
a young woman sits,
lost in a thought
that fills her black eyes
and shaken face
     with ... what?
What searing key to an obsessive question
that came to her in a drift
toward clouds of dream
by the half-mown field

and thrust her so awake with astonished
pain?
No way of knowing
what makes her sit there
agonizing
in that blazing field,
more or less forever.

You stand back into the museum crowd
as her blind, pained face
disappears behind a wall of backs and cloth
as you walk through the maze of galleries

to the museum's shadowy entrance
where the nagging question of her face

follows you out
into the rain.

Love Is Love

Is it possible to love where one was not in love?
You look across at me, and I at you.
The table of forty years stands between us
polished with courtesies, burled with respect,
built of knotted oak for voyaging, each on our own,
cloud journeys through starlit darkness.
I smell the sea wind of those journeys
you made possible for me with the wave of your scarf.
Unlike the mantis, you did not kill me,
nor I you, in poisoned masculine need.
Like the rhinoceros and the tick bird,
we helped each other live; shielded
the other's arms of dreams were true
to the taut lines at our rudders and our sails.
Our winds blew. Some wonder at our mystery.
We have no answer for you. For each other
grateful, salute across the weathering air.

Where Are You Headed, Young Fellow?

"Where are you headed, young fellow?
You almost ran me over, you know!"
"I'm headed for a date with my girlfriend.
I'm sorry, but I really must go."

"Is that where you think you are headed?
Are you certain? Or is it maybe not so?"
"Where else? She'll be mad if I'm late again.—
Hey what's that?" "It's only my shadow.

"Rest a moment, you have time. There's no hurry.
You're young and it's spring, and your lady
Will forgive you, I promise." "You don't know her!"
"No, but I will, even so."

"You ask where I'm headed. Well, I'll tell you.
I'm heading for a country that lies
between winter and summer. It's got no name.
But I'll build there my house, and my life."

"It is hard to build in that country.
It hangs between rock and space:
love's summer and a winter called courage,
and Heart is the name of that place.

But that is not where you are headed,
at most you will visit and leave."
"So, where, old man, am I headed?"
"Oblivion. . . ." But the boy had run on, and lived.

The War Roads

From burning Louvain and the Chemin des Dames,
bloody Tanenberg and the Lemberg forts,
the Somme's smear against the chalks of Champagne,
they ride over the downs, the ridges.
through broken forests, villages
crushed like basketfuls of eggs,
across plains of salvage and mud,
by the burning cloth halls, cathedrals reduced to bone,
across labyrinths of trenches soaking with blood,
shit, piss and rain, leading to this
hour where senile children
play at dominion
across a map ripped from a young man's hand
and shredded until the sense we cannot read there
shouts incriminations still, death's highway
still visible, through just barely, in the washed-out ink.

W. E. S. Owen: Sambre-Oise Canal, November 4, 1918

Afterward—little spring become prattling rill
grown rushing stream through the Shropshire meadows,
flower-dappled, by damp shade trees
and fragrant fields littered with picnic laughter,
brotherly sniping, early loves and later loving, faith
won, lost, then won again, and then lost again—
until it stepped into the garish sun
above an annihilated plain,
and the cool water filled with the casings
of spent shells and the crimson tunics
of lost boys and the stench of war,
the purer air rent with shouting
and the drunken symphony of the guns—
after the witty and warm words flowing
from a young man scratching over his knapsack
by candlelight or gaslight
or a glow of Vereys and flares—
after the warm life and the flowing life and the life-like
    sea of words
opening on that other life that always happens elsewhere—
the single bullet riving the early morning air
on the bank of the canal where all that stream was flowing—

the stop of it all, in the mud, like a hammer.

A stunned silence in the throbbing of the guns.

An unbelief in a no choice but to believe.

So it—now man, young or old, no longer—falls—
like Nineveh, Ur, and rich Babylon—
back into the darkness,
a face fading into the waters of an infinite silence.
He was.

Asteroid

One day,
a rock slightly smaller than the city of San Francisco—
infinitesimal by galactic standards, but decently sized by
    terrestrial—
slammed into what would one day become the Yucatan peninsula;
did not stop till it had driven twenty-five miles into the earth.

This impact made a crater of a hundred miles,
and sent a hurricane of echoes ringing round the planet
as though it were an immense bell,
causing earthquakes and eruptions of volcanoes
as never before seen
while throwing up an obscene cloud of dust
that blacked out the skies for many months,
creating storms with winds
blowing hundreds
of miles
per hour,
the atmosphere running amok from pole to pole,
until seventy percent (to give an approximate figure)
of all of life was wiped from the planet we call Earth.

Some survived—
mice-like creatures, insects, spiders, algae,
worms,
creatures living deep at the sea bottom,
that needed no light, or even oxygen, to live,
and were barely aware of the devastation

visiting the surface far above;
and, last (one might say) but not least,
a single family of a group of animals that we call
kyory, konglong, dinozavry, dinosaurier, or
dinosaurs:
pajaros, oiseaux, Vögel, pititsi, uccelli, niao,
birds,
or their ancestors.
This happened three score and six million of earth's
revolutions around the sun ago.

There is now another rock racing toward the earth,
unless we stop, deflect it, or turn it to dust . . .

But it seems that we
are the rock
racing
toward us.

Even if it strikes
and wipes most of life from earth's face,
like the tears from the face of a baby,
the *pajaros, oiseaux, Vögel, pititsi, uccelli, niao*—
the birds—
may fill the world, one day, again, with singing.

The Darkness Under the Crowns

The shadows under the crowns of the trees

a moist sultry blackness

only in summer evenings have I ever seen it
really? really the dusk
is so surreal

the evening air as gray as a Magritte
where bowlers hobnob under glowing streetlamps

(was that laughter? I could swear it was laughter)

the frosted sky bright with yellow crayons

The Silver Clown

on city stoop
in silver crouch
in silver cloud
a silver clown

crouched in a cloud
in a droop on a stoop
he's down, the clown,
all silver found

in brightness dipped
from toes to lips
from skin and clothes
to silver shoes

he gleams he seems
all mercury
of tin and light
all metal bright

all silver bright
all light to see,
he says to me,
but not for me

how can it be
Sir Mercury
Sir Silvery
there's none for thee

my skin is lack
my skin is bright
my skin is black
in silver light

King Midas made
of all things gold
in silver drowns
the silver clown

Burning

The gods of fire—
they race through the woods—
they catch seeds and little beasts
and tiny birds
in their yellow hands—
they claw back the wood
broken from the forest—
they eat the towns,
cruel, bright, heartless,
lifting their faces and bellowing the sky
black—
taking the innocent down
with the rest.

Smoke in San Francisco During the Fires of the Fall of 2018

He felt vaguely guilty,
Irrationally,
whenever he took a breath that day,
because he was afraid
he might be breathing in
the ashes
of Paradise.

A Visit to Paradise

The silence is heavy as the shade
from the blackened trees that, in the irony of chance,
survived the blackened homes.
Sunlight penetrates like cautious fingers.
You hold your breath, intent and shy
as an embarrassed tourist.
The air is sweet with wet ashes.
Then a birdcall, here and there.
A sound of hammering
as a man works on a gutted garage,
a call across a backyard
by a middle-aged woman
as she tries to raise a ladder.
The cough and grumbling of a small truck
abruptly swallowed as it descends a backward valley.
A tentative laugh from a clutch of kids
still not sure the woods around them
will not sink a second time beneath a lake of fire.
An old man walks firmly toward you down the middle of a road.
He is smiling, bravely.

Fossil Dust

the dire wolf and the smilodon
leave their bones in the hands of the hills
where the ice of want meets the smoke of desire
and the petrels shriek and the albatross hangs
her ring of iron in the rafters of space
and the drifter called time shakes his rags in the rain
and the tusks in the back of the truck turn to coins
in the dreams of the weapons left to rust in the car
and the northern stars have forgotten how to weep

time is a leaf in the book of the shade
a pebble in a glass of water a smell
that haunts the flowers of Parnassus spills
across the shale of Helicon
and seeps through the loam of a young girl's dreams

it cannot be and yet it was
the broken schist of a god's scree
melting in the mouth of a dazzled fawn
the glint of a firefly in a frozen wood
the fantasy of the atom's fire

the mammoth sweats out his lugubrious fat
in a canyon of glaciers while a gang of boys
finger their way up the tongue of the mount
and kiss their flints and the thunder roars

time time oh memory

curling your fingers in the mud-thick field
true oh illusion illusion oh true
holding the mind of the moon as it sings
of the dire wolf and the smilodon
and the dust of fossils and queens and kings.

A Shop of Clocks

where each keeps separate time:
a mantle claims it's 8:16,
a little alarm 11:08,
an anniversary quarter to three,
a grandfather clock a minute to midnight.

A pocket watch, hung on the wall,
is stiff as a minister: six o'clock.
A little repeater with no arms
tells all times—no time at all.

The cuckoo in the cuckoo clock
gapes, startled, at a gutted spring;
the pendulum clock is still as ice.

The shop of clocks is gravely still;
it's odd to see so many a clock
and hear no ticking and no tock,

silent—if alive, asleep,
or mummies in old Newton's tomb,
dreaming of a life to come,
future rich with present and past,
relativity's repast,

as if in the pregnant movie pause
just before the bomb goes off,
and everyone in the audience holds their breath;
when, together again, they all shall chime.

This

When you go down in this frail barque
where the air is signed with the seagull's shriek,
and moths ring fire around the lamp,
and ashes draw a bitter breath,

and the shiftless snow swarms like bees
among the sleeping apple's boughs,

and the wind sounds through a chink
in the heart's ice, like a jaded horn
sounding afar,
then in your bruised, cupped hands

a delicate universe will emerge
forgetful of what had become
of fretful dreams of little boys
and young girls' hopes; though even then

the winter will enclasp in spring
the seeds of summer, fall's rains,
the bright fingers of the sun
combing the horizon's slow dusk,

and you will call from the clasp
of sleep and from this lullaby
(for, yes, it is a lullaby)
and hie your fist until it shakes
awake the eyes of the sleeping god

who blindly plants the wandering seed
over stone and hardpack field

he sings his crazy song in the wind
and snaps the branches of the childlike trees
and thunders above the cowering
valleys, fells the wolf and jackal,
fills the night with groans of bliss
and ghosts into nothing an intoxicating kiss.

And you will defy this and this
as you go down in your frail barque
that seethes on the bitter sea of chance,
defying this, though it wreck and drown you,
chaotic, in the shouting dark.

Mysterium Tremendum Fascinans in the Basement of the Museum of Contemporary Art Denver

Not a dozen feet long,
a foot and a half wide,
it shines in its rack
like a silver cigar,
a shining, shimmering flying cigar,
cigale volant,
with narrow, almost delicate fins
and a short black nose
to show it is not without humor,
perhaps an early postwar rocket,
even a torpedo.

That's cool, I say, to put it in an art museum exhibit,
even if it's a little dark
here.

Next to a diagram on the silvery skin of the casing of arrows
pointing up, down and rightward, there are the words:

CHOCK
AND
SWAY
BRACE
AREA

This, I say, must be where it wants to be hugged.

You snort at the joke.
There is an inscription nearby that reads:

301705-00
B61-7 TYPE 3E
ALTS 0
SERIAL P758
INERT

Well, that's a relief, I shrug and smile, and exhale, not realizing I had
been holding my breath.

A worn, old tag hangs attached to the rack.
Maybe this will be more informative, you say, as the two of us lean
close in, our noses almost touching, to read:

USAFM-Loan
1994-3206-0014
MK 61, MOD 3E, S/N P758
1994-625
Bomb, Nuclear

Who would have thought it would be so small?
you say in a very small voice.

What do I say? It is not printable

in a family newspaper,
though it rhymes with "holy writ"

as it rises from its rack, Shiva, Destroyer of Worlds,
and flourishes in the basement darkness its
10,000 arms.

CHRISTOPHER BERNARD

Seventeen and a Half Past Five

At seventeen and a half past five,
the clock on the tower of St. Peter's and St. Paul's
stopped.

At seventeen and a half past five,
the pitcher froze on the mound
and the curve ball, spinning, became
a ball of ice held between grass and clouds.

At seventeen and a half past five,
a petal from an angel's tear
began falling.

At seventeen and a half past five,
the envelope opened in the lover's hands,
and he never knew what her words burned.

At seventeen and a half past five,
the sound of a bell's ring did not fade.

At seventeen and a half past five,
he stepped out of the window
and now hangs suspended in the air.

Spiritus

When you see it, you will know.
The shaky camera, the kneeling
men in midnight blue:
they look at first as though
they are praying, pious
as three altar boys,
caught in an innocuous crime, perhaps
stealing holy wafers or consecrated wine.
But they are not.

The shaking camera stops,
and you hold in your breath,
like clutching at a hand,
not quite believing that you see
what it is you think you see.

Underneath their knees,
in the brutal sun,
a dark form. And a voice from the feed:
"I can't breathe, I can't
breathe! I can't breathe! I
can't breathe!" For four minutes and
forty-six seconds,
as the altar boys pray
in the shouting glare.
Then it stops. The video
stops. The voice stops. The praying
stops. The breathing
stops And you breathe,
too late. But you seethe, you seethe.

Revolutions

I began my life with a revolution.
I will end it with another.

The streets my youth first walked on
crowded with ragged young armies
armed with guitars and profiles
of a perfect Pre-Raphaelite beauty;
marching under shouting and laughter
and dancing and singing toward a future
we faced with a terrified hopefulness
and a wrath of betrayal; that our elders
had savaged with war, lies,
the poisons of wealth and power,
bullying us out of childhood into a freedom
we were not ready for—is anyone, truly?
into choice and revolt—so we were dancing
into the future with our revolution.

Now age faces us again, starkly,
with a choice that is unpitying:
rip from history the last centuries
that have led to our home's assassination,
to mankind's suicide and the holocaust of species,
clean the stables of power and money,
cut off the gangrenous limb;
or wipe the last million years into oblivion,
rub out the merely human
into extinction, and all the ark's animals

Noah saved into a thin line of ashes
that separates geological eras,
and leave a smear of green on our graves.
Remake the human world
or die; not singly, but all.

That is our choice. Nothingness,
or the future, is ours.   *Time*   We
are old as the dying.   *begin*s   We
are newborn.   *here.*

In the Garden

When he died, he was surprised to see
how like was the Garden to the country he grew up in:
a rolling land quilted with farm fields,
undulating with saddlebacks and dipping valleys
covered with woodlands and black soil
and views spread for miles. Four seasons
held court in a kind of sublime alternation—
summers hot, fertile, sleepy, dank,
profoundly green, with knotty
lady bugs, gauzy dragonflies;
the wet autumns motley in gold umber red
with skies bottomless wells shadowy with daydreams;
winter stark with ice-sheathed woods,
the high ice-clouds vast frozen wings;
the spring ecstatic as a resurrection,
the scented flowers and grass an intoxication—
each season its own paradise, a promise
to return it did not betray.
Each day returned its expected favor:
the rising sun a silent fanfare
met by birdcalls lonely choirs
unapologetic courtiers of the emperor of day
as he entered the blue courts, clouds surrounding
like workshops in a sky-blue quarry;
the day advancing, steady
as the sun rode his dhow across the blueness,
each moment fresh
as a wilderness, dependable as a trusted animal,

nothing after or before exactly like it,
time like flakes of snow; passing the meridian
where shadows precisely meet the contours
of their makers; then the slow descent,
to the hour where beauty possesses the world
in a brief clasp, and the sun pulls down the sky
with a magnificence even greater than its rise—
and promise, love and hope are drawn upon the skies;
then night opens to the ocean spread behind the sky,
an infinite sea we call the universe;
and the moon embarks with her sad face half turned
from the sun's far horns of joy, and moves
silent and still across the dark water,
stars sparkling like waves, sea horses dancing.

Just like the world he knew in childhood
was the Garden: the people he met all family
or close friends, good fellowship wherever he turned,
kindness, grace, laughter, and dancing, and music,
fragile beauty, glittering, marbled cities,
and love, with quiet teasing and just
enough tears to make the next joy sweeter still.

This was the Garden. It quite surprised him,
as he had known it all his life; indeed, he had lived
there once. He had lived there always. All he had needed do
was open his eyes, and keep them open,
and refuse to close them. The earth had been Paradise.

Schumann Symphony

(Trumpets and horns.)

Spring: Oh hear—my call—oh world, my home!

The World: We hear—your call! The traveler's home!

O Spring—rejoice us now!

The winter's brutal winds have gone:
The storm
Has wrecked
Its last
Redoubt.

Birds are flying from the south,
Perching gravely on the fence,
Appraising bush and tree, they scout
A place to nest far from the cat
Watching from the windowsill.

Through a crust of snow and ice
That kept asleep the summer's dream,
Earth's eyes awake
As sun perks up the daffodil
And turns every eye to him
Until the universe itself
Even beyond his sovereignty

Breaks into song by a German old

In love with his Clara, life and earth

> For a season; till
> The trees uproot,
> Valleys wake
> From a cold trance,
> And bears give birth,
> And mountains dance.

Spring: Now, drunk with joy, let all things dance!
Oh drunk with joy, let all things dance!

The World: Till giddy-tizzy fizzy-tizzy tizzy-giddy tipsy we'll be,
                All around
                We all fall down!

Spring: So drunk with joy, now all things dance.
                (For, drunk with joy, how all things dance!)

The World: Till everybody
                Finds this treasure:
                Love, like life,
                Is pain and pleasure.

Spring: Drunk with joy?

No! Drunk on joy!

The World: No! You're drunk
                  As a love-lorn boy!

Spring: For Spring is love!

The World: And love is spring!

Spring: Dance if you know this!

The World: (If you don't know, sing!)

Spring: We're drunk on joy, so let's all dance!

The World: Oh drunk on joy, so let's all dance!

Spring: So drunk on joy—

The World: Oh, drunk on joy—

Spring: Still drunk on joy—

The World: All drunk on joy—

                  Forever drunk

Spring: On life—

The World: On love—

Spring: On love—

The World: On life—

                     On life

Spring: And love

                     And life

The World: And joy . . .

(Pause.)

Spring: Oh hear—my call—oh world, my home!

The World: We hear—your call! The traveler's home!

All: O SPRING, REJOICE US NOW!

Poetry, Actually

> I, too, dislike it.
>
> —Marianne Moore

... made, naturally,
of those secret cats,
words:
proud, seductive, quicksilver, slippery
and altogether treacherous:
they never seem to mean what one meant them to mean
whenever, and whatever, that was.

Writing it (or "inditing" it,
as Elizabethans called it,
which always makes one think
that actually one is "indicting it")—
with the slapdash pencil
or more moral pen
(so much harder to erase,
hide one's
literary peccadilloes)
or tapping it out (as now) upon the spying screen
(NSA: are you paying attention for a change?
If not, what are we paying our taxes for?
Bitter the poet who can't depend on you, at least, for a reader!)—
after a moment of absent-mindedness
plucked awake by a cosmic ray
into a half-glimpsed aperçu
touched with a pity flawed with beauty,

which seduced one into a few grunts of syntax
and a little bouncing grammar
while stringing together bits of elocution
whose definitions one only half remembers.

Then—after dribbling, with here a crossing out,
there an erasure, there a deletion—
taking out and putting back in again the obsessive comma, again
and again—
and again—and again—

half way down a page so rudely deprived of its innocence
and, up to this rough-handling, quite minding its own business—

finally, after all this costive, verbal hugger-mugger,
leaning back,
raising to the light,
reading it over
with a critical sigh,
one's lips silently speaking each
adroitly chosen and nimbly placed
Wort, mot, palabra, word,
with, in the end,
a proudly
approving
parental
pride

(though only after removing those impertinently provoking and
quite impossible assonances—
we are long past the mnemonic prostheses
of Beowulf, Piers Ploughman, and the Pearl Poet)—
voila!

that delicious sensation—
perfectly shameful and quite embarrassing—
of having committed an act of

literary vanity
political incorrectness
intellectual pretentiousness
sentimental mawkishness
brilliance
or follishness

once again—

despite every (admittedly weak) effort to keep one's
blinding light
buried in the caves of humility
and the silence of never-having-been—
burying one's "talents" never having been one's strongest one.

And then that almost criminal urge, in fact as in phrase, irresistible,
to rush about like a proud toddler displaying his little body's first

proud excretion,
and slip it, with all the ordeal of civility and rich, shy pride,
under the nose
of one's dear, much loved, much abused reader:
another forgettable poem in the universal library (a.k.a.
    Google Books),
that chamber of echoes, blockchain links, coded traces, pixels
breaking up, spinning,
dissolving, fading away,
like entropy,
more or less,
forever.

Because, in the end, one realizes,
after everything one has done—
the decades bent over the page of one's life,
poking, scribbling, deleting, rewriting,
one's life, one' loves, one's follies, one's joys—
like an accountant at his books that never quite add up,
no matter how often he adds them, and adds them, and adds
    them—
that one has failed.
Again.

Windfarm

a phalanx of ghosts bolted to the horizon

dozens? hundreds?

enormous, off a thousand miles,
hypnotic as a chimney fire

indolently whirling

the train gives a hoot as it races across the valley

like Sancho, or is it Quixote,
dashing, with sword upraised, toward the future

Dispatches From Pandemia

The Great God Pan

"He lives! The Great God Pan—he lives!"
echoes through the woodlands of the city
(the city is a kind of forest now
after a wildfire has crossed it,
the black trunks stripped of boughs,
falcons nesting on the towers' cliff edge,
with creek beds hard as cement).
Shock-haired New York stares, empty,
past the Statue out to sea.
The echoes, rough as goat pelt,
stalk the uplifts, the veins
of river, the skin of salt flats, the itchy
flannel of Rocky and Sierra,
cross the Golden Gate National Recreation Area
between the horns of the Bay,
cross the gull-shrieking Farallones.
The city, paralyzed like Sleeping Beauty,
lies in lumpy shadows,
towers like surprised fingers
in shock beneath a rising and a setting sun.
Blankets of clouds pinkly lap Twin Peaks.
The spirits creep like coyotes from the urban brush.
The coyotes themselves are howling
at Greenwich and Powell;
if you listen closely, you can hear them.
A cougar sneaks warily
between the ball park and Russian Hill,
staring at his own ghost

in a dark store window.
These are no strangers to strange gods,
nymphs, satyrs, goddesses,
the theophanies of Europe.
He lives—the Great God Pan, he lives!
And covers the world with his goat-like hoof.

The Silence

The silence seemed delicious. No one would have thought
the streets could be so still.
The whiplash hum of the cables,
slapping and whining in the slots
or clashing, electrically, above the streets,
the moaning and whimper of the busses,
the gnarled complaints of cars,
the arthritic squeal of a truck,
vanished, like the crumpled quiet of barroom talk.
The barroom talk, too, silenced,
with the garrulous, loud Pandora,
the restaurant ramage quietened
to a held breath by the cashiers.
The tap-tap of a single pedestrian.
The whisper of the wind in your ear.
The buzzing of a heavy bumble bee.
The full-throated aria of a mockingbird,
blithely ignoring sheltering in place,
singing his heart out at the top of a tree.

Under the silence, a trembling,
the lifting of a finger
turning in the wind,
like a cock on a weather vane.
West. South. East. North. East.
South. East. South. West. North.

The City Is Filled with Birdsong

The city is filled with birdsong.
The low metallic grumbling
usually backing the brittle
noisings, chips of sound,
throat clearings of gear shafts,
the muttering deep hush
and shrill siren cries
wailing distantly
into the city's simulacrum
of quiet, stills. Behind it all
is actual, real—can one call it, at last, true?—
silence.

Listen.

The city is filled with birdsong.

Kind indifferent nature
blossoming with joy
above the human darkness.

Beauty is love.

April 2020

We walk the silent streets among monuments
dark as tombs of an ancient time
long forgotten, frozen in silly
selfies and worries
no one can even remember now;
older than memory a time
that ended a mere week ago,
a month, a day, an hour ago.
March was only an hour ago.
March was an eternity ago.
It is spring and the flowers are blossoming everywhere.

Silence passes over the streets
(the sole sound in the neighborhoods,
the operatic bel canto of an endless mockingbird)
like the ripples from a stone that falls
into a neglected pond. They expand
slowly over the besieged city
dark and cool at the bottom of the sky:
over the clumps of office towers,
the chasmed streets, the glistening rails,
the darkened restaurants and bars,
the wordless cafes,
the tidy, disappointed sidewalks,
the hush of missing crowds,
the intersections of empty crosses,
the stillness of the churches

where the stoney bells ring above naves,
storefronts closed behind their shields
of plywood painted gray,
white, black, as if to say,
"We are at war, our ships are gray,
our will is black, our hopes are white,"

until they splash the hospitals
and there break
with desperation, grief and fear,
and the stone that is held against fear,
skill, courage, will, the hard
love of a determined yet frightened intent,
arrayed against an insidious invasion
riding the air like gossamer,
defending as with ax and pike
or mangy hides of a long-dead age
and howls of execration and rage,
the pierced wall of the modern town,
what now appalls the world.

Just yesterday, before the stone
fell, life, it was so much simpler . . .

That will be the future's myth.
Of course it will be a lie.
Life was never simpler.

Man against man, and against woman, was the rule,
commanded by genes, natural selection,
and our bizarre and human mix
of the irrational and the arrogant.
The world was, as usual, at war
with its silver-stained reflection in the glass.
Humankind was proving
a gorgeous catastrophe for life
on a planet the size of a pebble
thrown from a slingshot. We were the crown
virus enthroned in the breath of the world.

And now, in a cruelly fair reverse,
the crown virus has laid siege
to human monumentality
and mortified its pride. The skies
are clear of plane and smog, the clouds
and birds alone inhabit it,
the plains have only farmers cross them,
the mountains do not burn, the woods
are quiet with the stuttering of squirrels,
the tangled skein of interstates
is silent except for insouciant semis
running drink and food to the locked towns.
The night is black as ink
strewn with glittering points
we had almost forgotten.

The air, transparent for miles
as glass, stands fresh as morning.
Greenland freezes a film of water
back into ice. The corals
hold their limestone like a breath
beneath a glassy sea.

The city is filled with singing
and archipelagoes of blossoming flowers.
Birds, knowing nothing
but the leaning sun's ecliptic
and the burnished weathering of the wind,
migrate in their clouds northward,
choiring.
The flowers proclaim that beauty
will always triumph everywhere.

"We must love one another or die," said the poet.
Then changed his mind to the obvious fact:
"We must love one another *and* die."
But this thought undermined his poem.
And so he scrubbed the line, almost
tossed away the poem.

How
we live makes the change beyond
where we bow out of the light;

our choices made, our acts, our words—
these make our meaning, our truth,
our good, our evil:
the stones dropped in a pool,
ripples shivering outward
in growing circles of effect
into infinity,
the moment into eternity,
beyond our little lives more or less forever.

Must we die for the world to live?
This is the question with the forced reply.
If we say to that word "no,"
we are not free from what we know.

The Hammer and the Dance

The hammer and the dance,
in the atlas of the world,
in this season of pandemic,
like two stanchions on a court;
between, a tightening line
like the imaginary line
on the cartographer's expedient chart,
on one side, the dutiful girls,
on the other, boys in masks;
around them hung a wall of distance
that surrounds them like a fort;
at their feet, forgotten tasks.

And the hammer beats the time
for the young ones as they dance.

What of the future? What of the past?
What of the present? You well may ask.
There was something to be done
now forever left undone.
Where there once appeared a mask,
now a flawed map hides its face
in a hand scarred by this place;
now there is a face of ash.

And the hammer beats the time
for the young ones as they dance.

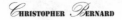
Deep inside the twisting globe
opens up a burning robe.
And tonight the silence hurls
into darkness its moot sign
like a banner never furled,
like the alchemist's alembic
charred with his defeated gold,
like the future's gathering dark
and the iron in the heart.

And the hammer beats the time
for the young ones as they dance.

Virus

The virus did not begin in the markets of Asia—
not the one I mean.

I need to go far back,
and move my finger across the map
to the west.
Tashkent, Ur, Padua,
Birmingham?
Or not so far: an Ionian isle?
Or like an olive greening in Galilee?
Or pressed under foot in a tub near Athens?

Wherever. It mutated
in the dust in the air,
stuck to a sandal, a plough,
hitchhiked on a rake, a veil,
slept in a vat of dye
or a krater before the wine slipped in
and dazzled the nose
of a prefect of a province,
a legion's general,
a senator toasting his emperor,
or the princeps himself, or a treacherous Praetorian guard.

Only later did it seed a barbarian's beard
and gather across the alpine mountains
north.

Its spores dusted the floors of the monasteries
and ministering cathedrals for centuries,
before the final mutations and hybrid
found its Frenchman, Italian, Brit,
and roiled now finally into plague.

The gaudy monster erupted down the centuries,
killing as it went—not its hosts
yet (it was still too clever for that)—
only the rest:
it became its host, and covered the world
with signs:
power, wealth, swiftness, conquest of land,
sea, air, space, time; threatened
death itself. The world shakes with its fever,
the steady drumbeat of billions of tiny earthquakes
pacing the crust of the earth,
as the temperature rises up the fatal scale.

It was a matter of time only
to meet its match.
Begins now the war of contagions.

What Are You Willing to Die For?

For Lt. Governor Daniel Patrick, of Texas

But what am I willing to live for?
The question haunts my ear
and stands, mute, on my tongue.

The crisp light of the sun,
the taste of the fragrant vine,
the dance of the music in my hand,

the slurry of night over the land,
the smell of Bucks County snow,
the shameless quest for love,

the austere idea.
The father's nobility
before we learned his truth,

the mother's love and grace
before she grew to myth.
The Tower of Babel of man,

the secret power of woman,
the boy's innocence,
the ice's solitude,

the hanged man of the moon,
the sun's diamond choirs,
the stars' cold kindness,

the haw of the wind.
The ranks of worlds in play
like chalk across the darkness,

the cars of books that sail
in separate galaxies
hurling from the mind,

a philosopher's cocked eyebrow,
a poem's tender shock,
a painting's seducing grin.

These I am willing
to live for. For what would I die?
For this, never:

to build a billionaire
from rocks of sweat and greed
(the sweat of fear, the clownish

dizziness of greed)
engrossed in a luxury
ripped like charity

of self-defeat, quite gaudy,
turning the sweating earth
into an infinite pile

of zeroes cleverly spun
from a wily algorithm,
the future into a dead

forgotten history.
In a time of plague,
the warning hour of nature

tolling above the cities
as she thrusts us aside,
in shyly frightened distances,

praying the curve will flatten
the arc of collective disease
like the arc of an enemy arrow

into the flight of a sparrow.
No, I will die
not, Lieutenant Governor Patrick,

for a commercial fee,
the toss of the dice,
the exuberant lie,

the proud god of "me"
that defines the broken heart
of the American economy.

On Wanting to Shatter a Screen

I miss it: the rolling eye,
the quick laugh, the joke, the grin,
the scorn at the news, the soft look
of sympathy, the amiable
shrug, the sigh, the shake of the head,
the crisp sound of shoes on the floor
and the comfortable walk into the room,
the room's echoes, its scent,
the texture of hair, skin, clothing,
the handshake, the shared bottle, the passed
bowl of chips: reality.

The tiled thumbnails of online imagery do not make it,
nor the seasick bursts of video chat, the odorless
echo-sapped chatrooms in the cloud.
The ghosts on the screen
seem to belong to a life I have never known,
nor wish to know,
like watery images from an uneasy dream
trying hard to look like life itself,
but fooling no one.

It is as if, after one clicks off,
the room savoring of the stale cigarette smoke of nothingness,
it is as if they were never there,
or only there to mock us
into believing we were ever there.

CHRISTOPHER BERNARD

Like memories of one's dead,
they look real enough to touch
if you could just reach far enough,
yet you cannot break through the glass to reach them,

When the screen goes dark, the room feels even lonelier.

And I escape outside,
walking fast through streets
that are empty and silent
or only dotted with a few people
wearing masks.

The Coyotes of North Beach

Sunset, spring: a strange wailing
rises from the gorge under our house
cautiously balanced on a cliff edge
as on a knife
above a valley where coyotes are gathering.

Strange indeed for a city
(our neighborhood, part declivity, part escarpment,
is strange enough for any city).

But maybe not strange for a city
largely emptied from a malady
emptying much of the world—
and giving meaning to the "pan"
in panache, panama, panjandrum,
Pandragon, panic, pandemic—
and so giving way to wilderness
seeping back into the streets,
crows appraising the roof tops,
mountain sheep strolling about in Wales,
curious spiders measuring bus shelters
with their delicate silks,

coyotes gathering at cross streets
and dancing in the glimmering streetlights
as they flicker on in the dusk
and making their coyote-like noisings,
as sweet as they are uncanny,

in the city's deepening twilight.

Why are they wailing so?
Is it from fear, or loneliness, or need for love?

How do the coyotes know
that they are speaking for us?

The Mockingbird

Alone, he twitters perkily, singing
away, chirping flirtily,
warbling scales, trilling like a diva,
at the top of a cedar's cowlicky branch,

blithe as a lumberjack in a shower.
So desperate for a mate?
Or just boasting his guarantee,
the triumphant domination of his tree?

The crows scare him off
(I've seen two or three),
but he comes back anyway,
so small, in contrast, inscrutable,
against their shining warnings.

He's the neighborhood's only success.
The people in the streets wear masks like hands
hiding their mouths and eyes
and scurry into their holes like mice.
Almost nothing else is heard
for days, for weeks, for miles, under a sky
locked like a cellar door above our heads.

The silence is like an invisible fog.
Yet it carries his message far and wide:
"I'm alive, alive, alive, alive, alive!"

Urbi et orbi

Myself, I prefer a city with no one in it,
or, if not exactly no one, only a few.

It's like being in an enormous sculpture garden,
immense minimalist slabs
of glass and concrete throwing shadows
dark as poetry across streets grown modest
with stillness and opening trustingly as a child's hand.
The few people there look less grotesque
when teased out of the crowd—
the way a solitary farmer turning his field,
a pair of friends or lovers, a daydreaming
hiker, seen in a summer countryscape
between bays of woods and folds
of pastureland and field, under
an ingenuously immense sky
make the dignity of humankind,
its vulnerable nobility,
palpable, and not the poorly spun joke
it seems so often
in a city hysterical, delirious and crammed.

No: our monuments, our things,
the traces of care in the woodwork,
the shadow of a mind molded from a sun—
tools and toys and trinkets, engines and edifices,
in a paleolithic cave the shape of a hand,
or a flute fluttering shyly, on an Easter morning—
make me less ashamed of being human.

I wander the empty city like a hunter
in a wilderness, except that I have found
the object of my hunt, and hold it close
inside my coat, where I can feel its heart
beating, and its warmth and its wings.

Social Distancing

—May 2020

Yet you have been practicing this all your life.
You've always kept a little place
as far as you could from the human race,
preferred your own company by far,
with cat, book, music, a little mood light,
with pleasure in the dusk,
with dreams in the night;
felt lonely only in a crowd,
such as one finds in those torture chambers of the spirit,
a party of strangers,
a bar after midnight,
team sports, parades, armies, group meals;
you are just someone who never feels
completely lonely alone.

And now the world, in its viral distress,
is joining you in your solitariness.
A paradox! But it mocks
neither of you, I must confess.

When you walk out to the city streets,
it's like being inside your own room,
if with expanding walls and floor,
enormous windows, thrown open door.

The city is quiet and empty and free,
filled with a monumental tranquility.

In a certain sense beautiful and true,
like walking about in an empty museum
peopled alone with magnificent work,
the city seems to belong to you.

The richest man is the one who owns
nothing, they say, and wisely, too:
the world before him is both his home
and his wilderness. (Another paradox!
They're as delightful as they are unorthodox.)

Your soul expands to meet a place
that knows no boundary in space,
city, country, sky, room.
You grasp your peace like a held stone
that hugs your pocket like a charm.
In the empty, still, and gleaming town,
you feel the fleeting grace of a universe.

The Dolphins' Names

Quick, sleek, blue, finned,
a joy of dolphins
slicks past the wind
jammering off the maiden prow
thrummed with the sheets
vibrating like a harp's strings now.

The scientific word is this:
they call each other by their names.
Why does this warm my heart? Is this
the word I needed? Does the world have names
and speak, and hear them, one by one?
Has each its own, a mask, a sound,
that points from each and knows its own?
Do the dolphins play their tune for one
and aim to say individuum?
Is the world uncanny then, not one
alone, but many curled in one,
a world of rhymes and glass, of bows
and curtsies formal as an old dance?
What are they speaking then? I bend
across the rail and listen through the wind.
"You are not alone. You are not
alone. You are not alone."

Faust Closes the Books on the Modern Age

CHRISTOPHER BERNARD

Faust Stalks the Streets of Katowice

The last time I was here, it was the Middle Ages
(Hey—the "middle" of what? You can ask that again!)
I rode the hump of an old woman
as she went in to town to market her vegetables
on a cart between her dog and her chickens.

The children in the streets were not kind to her,
children with something they have no more:
a future. For I was bringing the future,
full of magic and gold and power
and the first hint of the darkness that was coming:
the shadows beneath my cloak trailed behind me
like a wedding train.

For now we know what we were in the "middle" of,
what was before us, what behind:
behind us was this: the hope of the future,
going back long before the Greeks and Romans,
to the savannahs of the beginning, and our African home.
Before us was this: a loss like the wind—
before us was this: the beginning of the end.
I am the modern magician of the end,
I whose name in your crude tongue means "Fist,"
as I ride upon the back of your children.
At the time we were only humiliating an old woman.
Now we have finally reached our destination.
And now we shall destroy everything.

Faust Takes an Aperitif in Paris

Ah yes—those were the days. Days of hope,
you must admit (though the Dubonnet
was not so sweet, *n'est-ce pas*? I'd try
the Cinzano; it still tastes fresh! Unless
you like a drink that tastes like a summer soldier's army boot?
In that case, you must take the Fernet!)

Where was I? Oh yes! *That* Paris! Well, our leaders
at least pretended that they knew that we might have a problem
of maybe roasting the world up like a burnt turkey
with spoiled giblet gravy and bad wine
and a rancid pumpkin pie to make one die.
Well, all of us, really. And so they agreed
to keep the numbers down—not two—just one
and a half degrees (Celsius, don't you know),
to keep Greenland, the glaciers of the Alps,
Rockies, Andes, Himalayas, Antarctica,
to say nothing of the entire Arctic, from melting till
London, New York, St. Petersburg, Shanghai,
Hong Kong, to say nothing of Miami,
the Solomons, Seychelles, Maldives, Palau,
and Venice—well, Venice is going to be gone
whatever we do! Bye, bye! "Venice, Venice—
when thy marble walls
Are level with the ocean, there will be ..."
etc., etc., as Byron opined so ... byronically!—
till all those glorious, and inglorious, places,
those sonorously named and misnamed spaces,

sink beneath six or seven meters
of sea water.
They really made me feel—
those leaders of the world—that maybe I
had failed somewhere. Hadn't I
drilled them hard enough? Had I spared the rod
and spoiled the child? Had I failed
to beat the natural altruism out of their souls?
Had I unleashed them on the world not quite
clever and vicious and greedy and selfish enough,
in spite of everything I had done,
to say nothing of "Santa's little helpers": Machiavel,
Nietzsche, Max Stirner, Ayn Rand, Margaret Thatcher, etc., etc., etc.?
But not to worry: they had even me fooled!

I forgot my very first lessons: perfect the lie!
Always keep handy a vial of crocodile's tears!
And promise them anything! The people will believe
whatever you solemnly promise, as long as you
hunch forward in a little stoop, speak hesitantly, modestly,
but with jaw clenched with purpose, and pinch your eyebrows
in that hang-dog sincerity look memed all over my greatest
contemporary invention: the internet! (It was not Al Gore,
but Faust who invented that infinitely malleable
prison of the human mind!) Look now!
How many years later?
Nothing of any use has been done!
Cheaper solar panels? A few more forests of windmills?

Recycling in cafes?

Pah!

We're right on track to break through 3.5 degrees (Celsius!)

by 2050! The Sahara will extend from Oran to Brazzaville!

The methane in the tundra will start popping like a teenager's
pimples!

The northern polar ice cap will soon be free of ice by late
September!

And then—it's off to the races!

I knew I shouldn't have worried.

But you know me: Nervous Nelly even at the best of times.

I never believe the worst until I see it.

And now I see it plain.

Temperatures are breaking all records on the Champs-Elyseés!

The rain, when it comes at all, is sulphuric acid in the main!

And the Seine is as warm as a summer day in Spain!

Garçon, garçon! We're done with Dubbonet, Cinzano, Fernet!

It's now time to uncork the Veuve Cliquot and drown
ourselves in Champagne!

Faust Visits the Tivoli Gardens

So much fun! Look! The Star Flyer! The Demon!
Aquila! The Elf Train! The Chinese Pagoda!
The Dragon Boats! Fata Morgana! Tilt-a-Whirl!
The Sky Dive! The Plunger! The End of the World!
I always shed sixty years whenever I come here!
Buskers! Bangers! Lights! Night carnival of the cities!
It's Walpurgisnacht for Mom and Dad and the kiddies!

I haven't had so much fun since Charles
nearly fainted when I brought Hell
to dance half naked around his throne—
those demons can work it—man, what a thrill!
That song keeps going through my head,
though my memory made up the second verse of it:
"Wonderful, wonderful Copenhagen,
Life is there but a dream . . ."

The Little Mermaid, stolen once—or was it twice?—
and replaced each time with a sadder face,
as though she knew there was no more time,
droops so beautifully on her stone.

I almost wish I had not come
to Denmark, where all princes come
who mutter poesy while the murderers dance
at the foot of earth's darkening throne,
and life is no longer a dream.

Faust Leaves His Heart in San Francisco

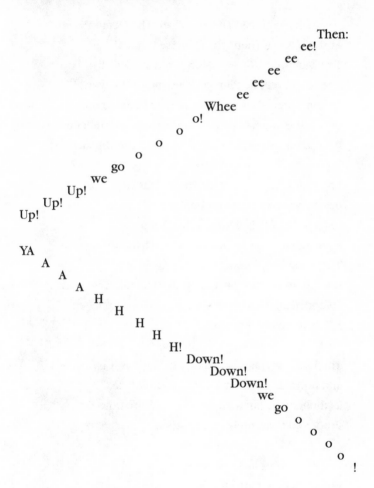

Wait—let me take a selfie

with Alcatraz in the background!

Too late! We've already swung up Russian Hill!

     and up
Over   and around
        and down
and upside down
(I'd swear!)
then down
       down
          down
and spun around

so we can do it all over again!

Now this is my favorite invention! Yes!
Faust invented the cable car,
as well as everything in the Musée Méchanique,
the Camera Obscura, and Laughing Sal,
and Irish coffee, and sour dough,
and ferries, and foghorns, and suspension bridges—
and the noirest city in the deep movie fog—
and don't get me started on Silicon Valley!

But this is the one I love most of all.
It matches exactly
the surge and fall of Father Time.
Otherwise the City of Saint Francis
my polar opposite is:
it believes, no matter the piling up
of disappointments
into the Angel of History's junkyard,
that man is good,

and woman better: it's quite incorrigible!
That city believes in its heart it can
save the world from itself—and me!
Imagine! [A list of current and impending
global disasters follows here.
We will not trouble the reader with
what they have read no doubt once too often.
Nor with our hero's tasteless gloating.
Just read "a baker's dozen of world-ending catastrophes"
        and continue.]
Such children! So hopeful! So clever! So blind!

If the entire world were like San Francisco,
you and I, my dear Mephistopheles,
would have very slim pickings indeed.

But never will they acknowledge this
little, uncomfortable, nasty fact:
that they are humanity's spoiled children.
Their way of life is an anomaly,
an aberration of place and time,
a perfect climate (ah!) in a perfect geography,
a perfect historical piece of luck,
and a conveniently placed silver mine
found by humans just when they needed it.
San Francisco the opposite of Death Valley is:
the Golden Mountain, as it was called by the wistful Chinese.

Let them dream. It is charming to watch them march
up and down the streets, shouting slogans and smiling,

convinced, if they just dream hard enough,

they will save the earth.

Such innocence! Such sweetness! Such folly!—Oops!

There goes the cable car grip

as it locks on the cable! Hold on! And it's up, up, up—up!

Look! The Golden Gate Bridge! The sun blinding off the Pacific!

History is peaking with us! What a spectacular view! You can see
    the world!

We will soon be at the top of everything—

then

    d

     o

      w

       n

         d

          o

           w

           n

            d

             o

              w

              n

               d

                o

                w

                 n—

and the screams of all humanity will tell
that we are being hurled to hell.

Faust Takes Command
of the Titanic

... as only seems fitting, as I
was a prime instigator (not to be
violently vulgar) of the birth of this epoch:
the final act of the Tragedy of Man
(and of Woman too, to be fair) that began
a few short centuries ago,
and now
promises to end with a fitting whimper:
a planetary desert covered with beetles
and oceans of pond scum after the methane comes.
What Faust began with my bargain with the devil,
Titanic ends in the frigid seas:
bookends of myth for modernity—
between great minds like Bacon, Hobbes,
Newton, Kepler, Mandeville, Smith,
and my favorite sage,
Tycho Brahe of Lüneburg on one end,
and on the other,
geniuses like Lenoir, Edison, Einstein,
Friedrich von Hayek, and Edward Teller—
those gods of our age
who prepared what we now know was always the end,
as man (helped by his better half)
took his fate in his hands, and,
with the power of a god and the wit of a fool,
prepared to destroy everything in his world.

I started it all,
in my study, with my philosophy
(whoever said philosophy was a waste of time?
The entire modern world came from a philosopher's brain!
   [he bows]).
On my puppet stage when I toured all of Europe,
with my veiled, Helen
and my pact with Satan,
and my miraculous deeds,
power, wealth, antiaging,
beauty, glamour—the bomb,
I modestly admit I was, as I led
science, invention, capital markets, wars
to conquer Nature and remake it for Man
(and Woman too). We rejoiced in my power:
I was, and am, the machine that drove
what we quaintly call the modern (who would have guessed
those appalling conservatives and reactionaries were right
about quite a few things? "Modernity is a pact
with the devil! You mark my words: it will turn out
badly in the end! And then you'll be sorry!"): that curious
and volatile blend
of cleverness, will power, false humility to nature
(like a player who only pretends as he flirts
while he drives toward conquest and dominion), arrogance
and desire gone round the bend with greed,
a drive toward absolute power

that can only lead to absolute annihilation
(a Greek tragedy where all mankind is the tool
to show the hubristic is the ultimate fool),
and a blindness that his very success
deepens to a darkness
deep as the blackness behind the stars,
an ignorance of himself that ticks like a bomb
toward the Samson shout that will bring down the temple
and raise over his head a monument of trash
obscene as the plastic gagging a sea monster
as blameless as the seafoam.

                                      I am that blind man.
Which is to say I have taken command
of the Titanic. I am a little ragged,
I admit, and wear somewhat outlandish clothes,
to be toffing about on the HMS bridge,
giving orders I barely understand, but the owners
seem hardly to notice, or even approve
as I scorn the cries from the watch of a shape
that looks, they claim, like an iceberg ahead.
But I know it is nothing. A bit of a cloud
with no more substance than my phantom Helen
or the other conjuring tricks I took
across the bankrupt market towns of Europe
still bleeding from the Thirty Years' War,
or the Peasants' Rebellion, or the Black Death,
or the fires of London, the burning of witches

and heretics, the Albigensian crusade,
or the tortures of man and nature put to proof
to give up their secrets to help mankind gather
the fardels with which to burn down the world.

But look, the moon breaks
above the ship's black row of smoke stacks,
and the sea all around us gleams with its light.
And there, bearing down on us, huge as the hills,
the one hill of ice my magic can't kill,
nor my pride nor my wit nor my power nor my will.

Satan, you have come. My name on that white writ
is signed, and sea, earth, sky are blackened now and forever
    with it.

Señor Despair
and the Angel

Señor Despair and the Angel

1. Señor Despair

Sand, evening.
The silence of the steps
as I walked down the breathing shore
after the terrible thing
I believed in too late,
for which there was now
only grief and despair.

The steps slip into, out of hearing,
a memory out of reach, a word
at the back of the dark mind
that will not come as I stumble over the weathering
shore through fog hiding the wide scape and my shame
behind a palpable grayness,
toward pilings that loom like the back of a crowd
in a dark theater as they wait
for the performance to begin, a tormented dance
to dazzle them
in cruel wordless patterns bound to something almost holy.

A shining crow—
rara avis indeed here where sea gulls usually rant and
    tangle,
smudges of squealing gray and dirty ivory, and quivering
    sandpipers,
and alcatrazes like cracked schists, loom—the crow
starts up, cawing and strident. It was too quiet anyway

under the surf's thundering.

"Do you see the patterns of the raindrops in the sand?" a
    courtly,
old-world voice seems to say, behind me.
"They call it random out of their mathematical *despair*."

The last word is spoken as if it were a word in Spanish:
    "des-pa-eer."
I turn to see a small, older man, smiling, attired impeccably,
bizarrely formal for beach wear—perhaps an *hidalgo*
from Oaxaca, or a *patrón*
from the cultured banlieus of Buenos Aires—
in an old-fashioned white suit, an elegant, bolo tie,
his hair and mustache groomed and white as sea foam.
I half-imagine he has materialized from the sea.

"But we do not need to listen to them too closely:
we cannot build a life on the psychosis of physics.
If you follow any chain of logic to its end,
you end in madness." I almost thought he said next:
"Come, huddle in my arms:
the night will rage with the storm, the rain is hard,
it cuts like ice through the black air.
At some point the thrill of life's harshness and our pride
in conquering it through brain, tough heart, and will
collapses and even the strongest huddle
in the dark, shivering and longing for warmth
in a cold that knows no compassion,
like children as we begin and as we end." But no.
He stood there politely and spoke on,

his English lightly accented with Spanish.

"And the storm, *la tormenta*, batters still the house,
the flood waters rise toward the door, a tree collapses—
se derrumba!—under the winds,
shattering the windows in a distant part,
and long thunder moves across the sky
like passing gods.

"*Despair* of God, *despair* of the world, *despair* of men,
of women, children, self: so what is left?
Despair of nothingness, *despair* itself of *despair*!

"So this is where it led, our reliance upon ourselves,
our proud *individualismo*,
the vast, the exciting lie we lived so long,
fundamento of our civilization, our 'way of life,'
the city great and strong wrecked by a shiver
of the earth like the shaken fur of an irritable bear.
So much for us! Screens banging in the evening breezes!
Distant calls of boys on fields of play!
A bouquet of young girls frozen in a gale!
A dropped napkin hiding a lost coin.
The numbers of the lost were beyond our counting, it was
astonishing, when one thought about it, which one did not
unless the bear breathed in one's face! It was terrible,
beyond possible imagining:
we had to hide it
from the children, from each other, from ourselves,
just so we could live on. It was very unscientific,
of course, but then science has many uses, like—

cómo se dice?—a Cuisinart does,
chop-chopping, as only it knows;
its every idea awaiting defeat by the next challenger!
A basis for belief is, alas, not one of them.

"Listen to the wind—*el viento!*—as it roughs up the house."
He paused, as if to listen to a wind that was not there.
"The next blow will flatten us, no doubt,
or if not, rip a hole in the sky
that will sink the world in the night like the sea.
It will be, as they say, very impressive!
I cannot take much more of this, being an old man,
and yet I must, foolish and weak as I am.
There is little tenderness, because there is little forgiveness.
I will pray to the night if I can find no other god.
But I can find no other god—*eh*, what of that?"

He looks toward the tumultuous waves still visible in the
    dusk.
" 'Join us!' they call. *Las sirenas*! Bandages over the eyes
of the blind to keep the light in before it
curdles like spoiled milk, bad
in the whites and the blue,
the tear in the iris, *el ojo distorsionado*, the blow
a la cabeza, a forgotten massacre, a scrum in the brush,
the irresistible *beso del tiburón* of certain smiles.
The crack between the night and the dawn
leaves much to be desired; nevertheless,
in a hundred ways we drop, in our parachutes, to the sea,
asesinos del sueño—assassins of the dream!
They could have been hoisted, though they never are,

as high as palm trees, helicopters, sky larks,
mountains packed with riches
like fat *chimichangas*. It does not take much
to score off them: they are not that clever, or tough,
just armed and charming. They are not afraid of blood,
just of being followed or recorded on their *móvil*
and unmasked beneath a job interviewer's grubby hands.
Near midnight. Ten and a half years in the future.
It was so hopeless! *Pero muy entretenido*! How you say: but
    very entertaining!
'I think I will dance my twerk to my belovéd country.'
she told me, *con dulce*. I was, I admit, moved.
When you fry the egg, it is hard to keep the yolk from
    running.
Te amo, they whisper,
hoping no one hears, but the wind—*el viento!*—hears
    everything.

"Oh those were the days, my friend!
We knew very well we were young, but we did know how
    young we were.
The early millennium!
Flamenco singing between dancing phones,
Google and Amazon and the death of the book (hats off,
    caballeros)
and the digital apocalypse (*tan radical!*), terror of Luddites,
threshold to the future we swim in, so warm,
wondering, what is the fuss? We still could smell
the glue, finger the bindings, wash the ink
from our fingers, still knew what a thing—*una cosa*—was,
saw the shadow vanish around the corner

with something like suspicion,
even dread: were not so certain the future
was one long *fiesta* of stock options falling over us
like a rain of infinite, shattering *piñatas*!
But not to worry!
Something survived of what some of us loved,
even treasured (one does not always treasure
what one loves! You will learn this, my friend, with time):
the coffin passed across no man's land,
over the shell holes, *los cuerpos, los olores*,
and travelled to the other side of time
to caress the eyes and the mind
with the truths that we thought we knew, with the beauties
we thought that we loved.
We took heart! There was nothing—*no había nada!*—to be
    sure of,
even the darkest of our imaginings never quite
se materializó—what is the word?—*materialized*, however
    much
we strove all our lives to make them do so;
just as *la felicidad mintió*—how do you say?—just as
    happiness
lied to us with each of its promises,
so *despair* deceived with its nightmares.
Terror is no better a guide than hope: this joke
we call what we can find no word for
('being,' 'life,' 'the human condition'? Pah!
    palabras patéticas!),
but with finger pointing and a hand waved, dumb and
    tongue-tied,
at the omnipotent folly we were caged and harnessed in,

like a sensible worm trapped *en la cabeza de un loco*—
and yet the psychotic seemed to have fits of sanity,
decency, good nature, like a well-meaning *idiota*,
(we were all *idiotas*
to someone at some point—in the future, to everyone!)

"A hippopotamus rises from the swamp, sleek and shiny in
  the sun,
magnanimous as his mouth, the smooth white molars
prepared to bite and crush *un elefante*!

"And Señor Hippo says:
Yo como el mundo—I eat the world!—
the seas I am getting drunk on,
the ice caps nonpareils, the continents
like a nicely grilled *bistec*, slabbed, aged,
and hung in the cold of the unanimous human night.
'Well now, I'm feeling stuffed!' says a voice. '*Scuso* while I
  belch.
That Earth was a turkey! At least it served a purpose!'
And the wishbone slips from my fingers,
shoots away down the kitchen floor, under the table—
why, no! A mouse got it! It's running off with it!
How about that! I wonder what it will wish for?
No doubt for a bigger cheese, or a smaller cat!
Or it will raise it up like an archway over its little mousehole:
an arch of triumph to raise its spirits
when it is feeling bitter about the fate of mice."

The darkness is thickening around us, like a blanket,
but a blanket of cold. The fog

has swallowed my thoughts. I cannot speak.
I stare hypnotized like a snake at the old man.
He smiles more deeply, stares up at an invisible sky,
lowers his strange eyes back to me.

"Imagine: one day I was invited to a party—
there was much food and drink *y música*,
and beautiful and clever and friendly young folk, and dancing
all night, and romantic corners just made for kissing—
a wonderful party where everyone is going and I was
    guaranteed—
guaranteed!—to have the time of my life—
but there was one condition, of course (have you ever heard
of a wonderful offering that is offered without a condition?
After all, we live in a capitalistic society!):
no one was allowed to leave the party alive.

"Everyone knew the condition? Of course we did;
we were not born, as you say so eloquently, yesterday!
It was even written in capital letters at the top and at the
    bottom and
at regular intervals across the invitation we each of us
    received
in the postal mail just two weeks ago.
"But each of us was convinced, everyone believed (and to
    this there were
no exceptions! *sin excepciones!*) that *he* would be the
    solitary, the lone, unique survivor:
he would sneak out just before dawn,
when the death squads were scheduled to descend on the
    silent household

where the partiers were lying about, dead to the world or in
restless dreams after the exhausting night's festivities,
and kill them all in their sleep.

"But neither to this were there any exceptions,
though one or two were rumored
perhaps to have survived: Jesus, Ahasuerus, Cagliostro, King
    Arthur.
People are constantly looking for them:
they look into the face of everyone they meet,
hoping that maybe this one is a survivor.
I myself have been taken for such! I am certainly old enough!

"This is almost as jolly as a mouse's life.
He gets his strokes and pleasures where he can.
Poor mouse! How fortunate we are that we are not mice:
we have immortal souls
and will rise from the dead in the flesh (at least so the
    Christians say:
a system that seems, since we end up in the same body
we first ended with, *no muy eficiente*).

"Do you have a soul? You often wonder about that. I know
    this!
The scientists, those *nihilistas*,
are almost gleeful when they say they can't find any
prueba científica for it, so, like ghosts, fairies, and God,
it must be dismissed with a patronizing skepticism
and condescending doubt one gives for *idiotas*
the uneducated, and Republicans!

" 'Do pigs have wings?' Of course you do not have a soul.

That thing that aches in the space you feel
behind your eyes, between your pate and your feet,
and thrums with ache, squats with grief,
or shakes with joy and love
is nothing but ... is nothing but ... is nothing,
nada, though it feels it is
todo—all.
Like this fist."

           He raises his fist and looks at it
almost with admiration.

"It can build a city, it can kill
a rattlesnake. It can shoot a president!
It may be nothing, but it is a nothing that can make nothing
of everything, *si quiere*. Remember that,
my physicist, biologist, economist, psychologist, psychiatrist,
    capitalist, Antichrist.
Did I say that? I did not say that—erase it from your mind.
It was not said, it was not heard or thought or
dreamed. The truth will set you free
por nada. It opens the prison cell
to reveal *la prisión infinita* beyond.
Jesus was a liar. They crucified the right man,
though only *la gente honesta* knew it—and paid the usual
price for integrity! Hatred for eternity.
           We must be careful,
my friend: only the select have ever heard me this far
(they usually run away!), either they are willing to be
    corrupted
or they have the *espíritus fuertes* as antidotes
to kill the poison before it murders their ... souls. The rest

yawned off in droves: we have the stench to ourselves,
the sweet, sick briny stink of feckless fact
and pointless, useless
truth (*Sí sí! Esa palabra sucia!* That dirty word!
Go, *vete*, foul *escéptico académico!*
Back, back! Where is my garlic? I carry it on me at all times
for times such as this! Where is my stake
to thrust through thy black heart at dawn!
Where is my cross! The terrible count
must be destroyed so we may live in hope
of happiness, if not actual bliss:
Truth is dead! Long live the Truth!) For what are you,
my friend? A prince in exile, a sovereign on a burning throne,
a blind king in a republic of the lost.
Sí, mi amigo! I draw your face in ink on coal
against ashes and night."

The old man pauses and locks my eyes in his
in the darkness as it tightens softly around us.

                              "You think me *un viejo loco*,
scrambled with drugs and too much *tequila*—'crasy
    in the *head*'—
or just an outdated crank, pathetic, worthless. And you are
    right!
It is better for you to think so, you who are young,
however old you feel: compared to me,
you are a child, and deserve to keep your innocence
a little longer (if only it could be much longer!)
en las cadenas del mundo y del tiempo—
in, what do you call?—the chains of time and the world—

as long, that is, as you are able to deny them
in the furor of your inspired mind
and your strenuous will,
your pride and your fury
at the fate that world and time
are wreathing around your future, that you hope
to defy with a brilliant signature across the air
that all may see, or none, that shouts out *estaba*
     aquí—I was here!
Once, once only, irremovable
in the sun's cold memory, *para siempre.*
Even if no one ever sees it again: it *was,*
eternamente, like an absolute
matchstick—*un hombre: un fósforo eterno!*

"So what shall we call it, for we must have a name for it,
however *obtuso*, however *inadequado*,
For we must mouth a meaning for it, a word we can blame
     on it,
to give us the illusion of knowledge, power, use.
'*El Reino des Perdidos*'—'The Kingdom of the Lost'—I first
     liked then found *trillado*, trite,
then 'Ink on Coal' before I found that too *banal*;
'*Despair*' was at the head for a week; even better:
     '*Désespoir*'—
before my *crítico interno* returned, and put that in the
     pissoir!
'An Enemy of the People'—now that is an honest title!
And one without a bit of the too-poetic riddle one is so
     prone to! But Ibsen used it,
and people looking for a Stockmann will be unforgiving.

'A Prince in Exile' and 'The Plot of the Homeless
    Sovereigns' were desperate gestures only,
and 'The Wilding Masters' was an admission of defeat.
We eventually settled on an old unused name,
direct, simple,
and fitting the dark mystery of it all:
'*El Viento y la Noche*': 'The Wind and the Night.'

"I remember how the sun rose then.
It seemed to, how say this,
flatten itself against the winter sky
like a wet coaster after a truly bad party.
The throngs of clubbers staggered from a bar called The End
    Up,
cursing the feckless paradise of a dawn in California.
It was impossible: the morning was insistently gentle
as a doom of vodka and whipped cream, or mercurochrome
and lilacs: the blood removed beneath the nails
and the hammer resting, chilly, in the carpenter's box.
The heroes banked in a peculiar fire.
Bits of confetti were caught in their hair.
Monster Din met Monster Pan:
they bowed with a terribly earnest politeness
so that no one might justify a mutual goring.
It was damning: for only a murderous hatred
with a dish of poison and a shot of blood
to tickle *lo imaginario* could make a man glad.
Love be damned! It was hatred they were loving,
and the prospect of crushing an enemy.
Not the fact so much—the *idea*: a nice, solid dream,
une jolie fantaisie, as the French say,

that glows basking them in a brash triumph.
Here is joy; there, *despair*—
désespoir!—where certain defeat opens its chops,
bites carefully (watch out for the bones!), and munches us
slowly, to a hush of giggling in the next room.

"The world is not content just to destroy—no!
It must humiliate at the same stroke:
murder and jeer and annihilate
you and all your works. Truly a goal worth pursuing,
even if not entirely realistic! Who knows,
next time it may get it right!
The *Prince de ce monde* will be certain to aid you if you are
patient and humble, and persevere: perfect destruction,
is sane and beautiful as perfect creation—if not more rare
and more beautiful still—*más raro y más hermosa todavía*:
una perfección only the unknown can have. Like certain
    suicides:
a song, a drama, a dance,
in which realization, culmination, and ruin
are one. Are one. Are one. Are one.
The light is only another form of darkness,
an old *cínico* once said in my hearing.
'You are bitter,' a harsh voice, not mine, replied,
'only because you are a failure.' 'Not quite,'
the *viejo*—even older than I am now!—answered, tranquilly,
    'I am not
a failure; I *am* failure; I am not bitter,
I am *bitterness*.
I am a pineapple upside-down cake Midas;
I turn everything I touch into ashes and mud.

It was most perplexing until I discovered why:
My *orgullo—cómo se dice?*— 'pride,' called *arrogancia*,
'arrogance,' by some: cocky, conceited, prideful,
pretencioso, superior, stuck up; I have gotten them all!
My certainty of my own value,
my repudiation of *humilidad*, my detestation
of that miserable virtue called *la modestia*:
my self-respect grown thick with self-regard,
my insight, new every day, that, in this world,
the sun, the world, *el universo*, revolved *perpetuamente*
around *mí mismo, para siempre y en todas partes*.
There was nothing I could do about it.
Mi mundo era yo.
I was the world.
When I die, so dies the universe."

"No!" I want to shout.
But a mask of overwhelming tiredness
falls across my face. The old man sighs, but seems
not to notice, and drunk on its own eloquence,
the voice patters on.

"But courage, my friend! Courage, defiance, and wit: a taste
    for metaphors
and a sweet, mouth-filling phrase: much can be
made from the bricolage, the landfill, the pit
the cosmos truly is: a nest for imagining
a myriad earths,
unos universos eternos y infinitos,
out of the humus, compost heap, trash,
swelling like lotus blossoms from the waste

and perfuming the morning with a wilderness sweetness
none—no, none!—could have hoped for or dreamed of,
a delicacy exquisite, softest of elegance,
a living line, the profile of a rock
cut from a cloud: the hand of an angel
baffled, as it turns in the air,
by all the beauty floating across the emptiness
like waterlilies across a black, still pond.
And who is there to consider all this, delight
in its million brief enchantments,
its undomesticated glories, cozy, snuggling,
and quite comical smiles, its conquests, its gentleness,
its vagrant ecstasies, its barren splendor,
its mystery opening on all sides, without end—
who but us, my friend? And a few torn-winged angels
we no longer believe in, and a passle of other gods."

The sun had fully set. I could see no more than the old man's
    shadow
against the black wall of the sea, from which a voice
emerged; another voice in the wash of waves.

"Hating one's country, one's home, one's countrymen,"
this new voice (but was it a new voice? there had been so
    many voices,
or was there only one voice?) this new voice said,
"loathing the looks on their faces, the sound of their accents,
the rasp of their shoes on the sidewalk, the smell of their
    cars,
the general scrum for necessities they pretend is a virtue,
though it only proves them *unos esclavos de la realidad*,

CHRISTOPHER BERNARD

their power a fraud, their wealth tin cans and tinsel,
their glorious technology, computers, internet, science,
their conquest of space, their knowledge of the stars,
their clamoring for the heavens to finally descend
with godlike powers to finally grant them the most
extravagant wonders: subservient mirroring—at last
nuestras verdaderas almas gemelas—our true soul
    mates!—
the perfect shadow of our imperfect profiles,
our silhouettes against the hard, cold black
in which we hope to find our own, rude faces,
glamourized, at last, back to us:
a carnival of freaks, a laudanum delirium
as epic as creation, *un flujo de datos*—a data stream!—
become a deluge swallowing our dreams;
and fame a cruel substitute for a love
all want but none can give:
despising *este espectáculo extraño*—this freak show!—into
    which we were born
is both a sign of good taste and a waste of spirit—
for only pity sees the mask
breaking behind the brazen face
where fear fights with pride, grief
with insolence, folly with a fearful suspicion half carved
    from wisdom
and half from an incorrigible refusal to look into the face
of reality: the human spirit, part demon, part angel, part
    monkey—
the pretentious ape that invented God and hell
and fantasizes *un paraíso* inside his skull.

"I am caught between nausea and hilarity
at *la bestia* I cannot disown.

                                    "I cannot hate them,
though I often despise them
for not being better than myself. Who can I learn from,
if not from them? My own hopelessness I know
too well to depend on my *sabiduría débil*—
sickly wisdom!—my often ridiculous judgment,
reared as I was in bedlam and educated
(if that is the word!) in *este manicomio*—what you say, the
    madhouse
that is the world (I admit this to you
because you are *un extraño*—a stranger—
what I can admit to no one else, not even to myself!)

"But—you are right"—though I had said nothing.
 "Even more foolish is bitterness,
though it cleanses the soul to let it out,
like a scrubbing with a little black soap and brimstone.
It feels nice to rant, half mad, and say unjust and terrible
    things
to an innocent and long-suffering listener, a captive audience!
Like yourself, young *señor*! To hell (not to use stronger
    language,
but I have some respect for your sensibilities,
which may not yet have been corrupted
by the fashion in profanity that is now all the rage,
young *señor*!) to hell with this, to hell with that,
to hell with it all! One feels so much better afterward.
Imagine a nuclear cloud rising above the city:

it is like a shrine, a stupa of cloud and blood,
veined with lightning;
cleansing the world through destroying it.
There is a delightful, delicious word for it:
lalochezia! So luscious a word for the tempest of liberating
     profanities!

"Wherever I look, there is no matter,
and mind disappeared long ago
from every metaphysician's backpack. No mind, no matter,
just waves of energy crossing uncertain voids,
not even nothing underneath:
the only thing we know is words
that cannot even quite say it!
Which leaves me shipwrecked on a dictionary!
I cannot even *say*, *adecuadamente*, that I cannot *say* it!
I am a blot of darkness in darkness,
and light is no more than the wishful thinking
of a blind *loco*.
Do not be bitter (so I speak to myself); by all means, be not
     bitter;
you are not alone, cramped in your little cell
of body, time, brain—though one can feel
lonesome even in the mob
of billions that have joined one on the earth:
your fellow creatures backed against the night.
Do not let your self-pity fail to hold them
in its arms. They watch the same moon fail and surge,
and scrounge the sun's seeds from the brittle earth
and stare, like you, at the blackness behind the stars—
that strangely comforting blackness!

Unlock the gate that you closed, hastily and a little late,
behind your heart after, like a horse, it fled!

"The heart's fear masks its love.
Its hatred masks its munificence."

I raise my hands to my face in the darkness.
Somewhere someone is praying.
But only silence crosses my lips.

"Oh, *mi niño* ..." The voice almost whispers with
    compassion.
Or do I only imagine it? "There is nothing here to dispute,
no cause for debate or quarrel—unless of course
one's long quarrel is with God! 'He's too big
for that,' someone has told you. And
he had a point—though, you rejoined, only a man
without spirit would let so weak a reason
prevent him. God can stop the quarrel
the moment he cares to: oh, there is nothing simpler,
he only need give a clear and simple reason
for the world he made, and for *us*. Clear—*claro*—
above all: stop pretending we are children
and fools. We see through you. And do not think
you can hide behind the atheists. What a brilliant
ploy you thought that was! You do not exist!
Poof! You are now off the hook, and the nihilists
can go wreck the world between their bombs and bottom
    lines.

"The devil's cleverest trick was convincing us he was a fable,

and now you're trying it out on your own! Nice try, *o Señor*!
You must have more on your conscience than I thought!
The stars are sprinkling bath salt on the night,
to make us cry as it stings beneath such beauty."

The pause is washed with a blur of surf,
dimly white, like the old man's moonlike shadow.

"Let us face it frankly: humanity is a fiasco.
A once promising idea, in the chaotic mind of nature,
gone terminally bad. A piece of dumb luck, as your colorful
    slang puts it,
that has finally overstayed its welcome.
It is not nice to admit—not nice even for an old man,
who is supposed to be wise, gentle, not upset anyone,
unless he is a senile lunatic (then one can sneer and ignore
    him)—
he is not supposed to throw our trash in our teeth. Lie to us
as if you loved us! I can hear you even now,
your shouts drowning the waves.
Love you? Learn to love, and I will try to return the favor!
Man is a bizarre accident (alas, woman also, *siento tener que
decir*)—
and probably is alone in this chaotic cosmos:
just him and God! Two points of consciousness
and perverse will, one *mortal*, one *inmortal*—
talk about having nothing in common but thin skins
and a bad temper! Fourteen billion
years of grandstanding between them! What a farce!
Clowns performing for an audience of clowns!
Am I being cruel? Have you gazed with unjaundiced eye

at your neighbors? At yourself? You are not the exception.
What goes on inside your head, *en su corazón*?
Dime, what do you see there? No, don't tell me.
I have had enough *despair* for one evening."

A gull, pulled from the passing wind, screams
through the night. It's so dark, I cannot
see my hand in front of my face—
that is a true phrase.

        "Though the world seems dark, and is,
what good is there in dwelling on it? 'Cheer up'?
(As your Anglo cousins, with their stiff upper lip,
obnoxiously say.) Not yet! Tally-ho! Not quite!
The moon drifts up most nights even now,
the lapdog of the sun. The sun crooks an arm
and throws the earth into another round
del baile sin fin—of the dance without end. It makes me
ill to think about it. And so I don't.
If I attempted *pensar la realidad*—
how do you say—"think reality"?—
who could survive it
an hour, a week, at most let's say seven months—
yes, seven months!—before collapsing, shouting,
half crazy or dead, or more likely curled up like a little baby,
regressing to the middle ages of Ptolemy. As so many have!
El infierno is easier for some to take
than *el universo cuántico! el Antropoceno!*—the
    Anthropocene
in the quantum universe! With a gravy
of natural selection, the unconscious, brain chemistry,

the libidinal robot, the ego's comforting fabrications
that keep our secret psychoses at bay,
and a world, a world we cannot know,
only that it will, eventually, *finalmente*,
annihilate us. *Y todo en lo que creemos.*" Did I hear him
discreetly cross himself, or only imagine it?
"That is, if we do not—
eh?—what is your expression?—ah yes!—
'*beat it to the punch*!'

"You think I exaggerate? The truth,
which you believe does not exist, like God and the devil,
is poisoning his arrows at the edge of the universe,
that beige and brain-shaped cloud, before he notches
his bow. It will take less time than forever
to reach us, entangled as we are, like a ball
of yarn at the end of a day of a kitten's hijinks.
The claw is no less sharp and merciless for the sweetness
of the eyes of the owner. The world is lovely
just the same: innocent, beautiful, ruthless,
as only the unminded are. A lie?
*Dime una mentira para que pueda volver
a dormir.* Tell me a lie so that I can sleep again.
Too many truths have burnt a hole in my brain!
I hear the silence of the arrow—*el silencio de la flecha*—
as it flies toward me . . ."

2. The Angel

A drop of mercury pools on the horizon;
a pale bruised piece of sky fading above it,
and, curling from a darkness that has been only a voice and
    night surf,
I think I can see the old man
in his old world summer suit,
in silent profile, bowed before me.
                             "I think,"
I say, stumbling over the words, I have been silent
so long: "I think ... think maybe it ... "
The old man seems not to hear me. " ... maybe ... it
isn't as it seems to you: only horrifying."

He appears to raise his head. "You think ... ?"
he says, in a voice soft as an owlet's down.

"Yes," says my voice
surprising me, for some reason. "The world ...
the world, with all the ... its cruelty, chaos, its
brutal banality ... that ... everything you say is true, at least
it meets my own experience like the two ragged edges
of a broken bone:
the stupidity and suffering, much of it
caused by the stupidity (I have learned that lesson only
too well)—still the world has ..." I stop, a number of
hopelessly inadequate words beating like trapped birds
inside my brain,
trying to escape.

"Has what"? the old man asks.

". . . A fascination."

I bite the inside of my lip, waiting for the laughter
to crow over my insufficiency,
though the silence is tart as sarcasm.

"A fascination," I repeat, rather desperately.

"A fascination," he says, expressionlessly. "*Una fascinación*.
With what?"

                    "With the wonders. With
the magnificence.
From the smallest wave,
the tiniest of particles,
flickering, radiant, from the black hole's sucking zero
to the scattering spore of stars, the scudding black backs
of galaxies in their nets of dust, and who knows what
endless shoals of universes raised around us,
across or through us, even, in time and space
endlessly beyond infinity, forever
shaming our clichés of eternity like toys
cast off from a suburban nursery, and presenting us
with a terrifying glory,
serene grandeurs shining between tempests we never
       beguiled
in our mythologies, never knew were possibly available to
       us,
yet that may be only a poor man's

weak trial at conceiving a reality so far
beyond us it must make me worshipful
of the world that created me, created us, not we the world:
our world
as far beyond our largest notions of eternity and 'god'
as those were, have been, beyond us, any, ever or now:
yet nothing here more true.
We live at the heart
of an immense divinity without beginning or end,
and this divinity is the world.
We just did not know it before so … definitively.
It has nothing to do with God—it is beyond God."

"It is beyond Satan, you mean," the old man's voice says,
    softly.
"It is a beautiful thought. *Un pensamiento hermoso!*
But it is only a thought.
We do not live in the manors of the universe,
but in a hole where we sweat to make lives
in fear and cold, imagining the fire that does not warm us,
surrounded by rivals, in danger of failure, shame,
friendships lost for inscrutable reasons,
disease, old age, poverty, self-disgust,
failing to get little or nothing of what, or of who,
we most wanted. Our desire itself—*nuestro propio deseo*—
walls us from the enchantment: that loveliest of women,
esa brillante carrera, respect, admiration, love,
except in doses *tan pequeño* they are almost insults, proofs
of what we cannot possess. When, despite fate, you grasp
a trophy of granted longing, the envy of 'friends'

who will not forgive your shabby, little reward, poisons the
    air.
Wealth, fame, power, love are shelterless
from the envious—as our own envy
wounds our lives for success we have missed
and feel we have earned, with justice or without.
We stink to ourselves in defeat.

"Fate is a pyramid staring down at its climbers,
haughty and cold. When I lose that penny,
it is bitterer than never having had it:
like love. I would still have had my dreams;
now I have lost even them.
Success—victory—itself is shameful
if it means another's defeat. But that is how it works,
this glorious world you are so romantic about:
for every beauty you see, a thousand uglinesses
have been crushed,
for every glamour a powerless rage is paid.
You think you can try again, that the door is always open.
It is not;
the door finally closes, or has been always closed and only
    seemed ajar.
La vida es una ilusión fabulosa, invented to keep you
moving ahead in hope, deceiving but ever renewed,
struggling *como un gusano en un anzuelo*—
like a worm on a hook!—
working at a pointless job, putting up
with a mate you have never loved, producing
children who half appall you and wholly bore you,
spending much of your time trying to persuade yourself

your life is worth it, existence is a gift
that is not guaranteed to destroy you—
that your birth was not a white elephant. And yet, it is: *pero
    es así*—
it annihilates you, life, body, work, name—
and leaves just enough to mock your appearance here
on an empty stage under lights no one will see."

              The moon
crests the horizon, its face
of cartoon sorrow, round and full as a baby's,
glows bright silver porcelain in the blackness,
yet as though lamenting everything it sees.

"With all due respect, *señor*"—He bows in the opening
    moonlight.—
"don't you think you go too far? Don't you think
maybe you are offending
the miracle?"

          The old man does not move.
But after a moment I think I hear a gently spoken
question: "Miracle, *mi hijo*? *Que milagro?*"

                  "The miracle
of this shabby, this shameful, this dubious life.
By all the laws of chemistry, biology, physics,
relativity and quantum mechanics,
it should not have happened at all.
So, what if this
world

is the miracle I have sought,
the riddle I must solve,
pain that I—*I*—must overcome,
chance to build into meaning,
an ugliness to alchemize into beauty,
pointlessness and meaninglessness to loom
into love and warmth and joy,
a chaos I am dared to find patterns in?
My life—that bricolage theater for oblivion—
a smudge of ash in the next geological stratum,
a hiccup in a random turn of evolution's wheel,
until the sun
grows fat and red and devours the earth,
or, shriveling into a kind of icy kernel, freezes it,
or explodes and stars a far-off night
for an hour brighter than the galaxy. But not
certain is any of this, and the presumption that I
can know
what it is impossible to know—
the future—
is a peculiar crime of the human mind,
thinking it a venial sin;
and, since I
squirm recalling thoughtless hopes
that broke in my hands like eggshells
and left my mouth acrid and bitter,
I choose to tell myself dark, harsh,
cold and despairing truths, thus to avoid
another intolerable disappointment. But the same
compulsion drives me: the craving to know—
the need for knowledge when ignorance only

is to be had, uncertainty and darkness, for all of us are
    children
before the unknowable.
                      "Maybe it is true that I am
little more than nourishment for oblivion—maybe
it is *not*: I don't know either way.
I may have faith
that, since I am here, now, and have
in a little way thrived,
the world is not absolutely against me
or my somewhat abrupt arrival at the party.
I can go further." I pause. How
preposterous all of this sounds!
But I say it anyway. The old man
has not moved. "It supports me—it
encourages, shields, shelters, defends,
holds me,
holds me upright,
is me.
I am an expression of its power,
I too;
of the power that builds sense, life,
mind, good, beauty, grace,
against the power
arrayed against me: brutality, stupidity, destruction, and
    death.
The power poisoning the air. And it is my work
to aid the power that holds me in its hand . . . "

"But that is where the poison works
to most penetrating effect," the old man

breaks in, smiling softly, softly smiling.
"*Exactamente en el corazón y el alma y la mente*—
in the heart and soul and mind—
that you extoll so *extáticamente*. There the monster god,
loco, lunático, imbécil, aleatorio, brutal,
works at his most cruel. Life,
la vida es la bestia: life is the monster
that feeds on life, that digs down
to undermine meaning and joy—
a miracle indeed! *Milagro satánico.*
It was human intelligence that worked out entropy,
thus putting an end, *irónicamente*, to eschatology—
the study of final things!—
even better than the sainted Darwin.
Our science reveals merely the dimensions of our prison:
it is quite infinite. Have no fear! There is no escape.
The human brain has proven that the human brain
is an accident, and thus proves nothing—
more: it is an *aberración* that spins out fantasies
it feeds on and must believe in: reality
is ultimately not even—*cómo se dice? disponible*—
    available to us.
We crave for something we cannot have—
and so we numb ourselves with games and drugs
and art and music and philosophy and literature and religion
and wealth and power—*y el lujo y el sexo*—
anything to escape the intolerable gnawing."
Beneath the moon an immensely long, glittering spear of
    light
reaches across the ocean to the horizon,
as if pointing toward the darkness.

                                        "But aren't we free,"
a voice in me replies to the white silhouette against the
    darkness,
"to make, to find, meaning, meanings when we can?
Haven't we escaped many a horror of the past,
haven't we earned a right to hope for more?"

"We are free, it is true, of the artificial vise,
so now we can see the more natural chains,"
the old man, patient as a professor
to a new student (but not unpromising!) explains,
"That piping Emerson, that windbag Whitman—
what did it lead to? *Democracia, la libertad,*
America! Look at it, remember it:
there is a country that has no excuses—
and what has it done?
Mira! A nation half mad with greed, power-lust, pride,
a foolish, arrogant culture that parades
ugliness in the name of *libertad de expresión,*
an infantile denial of unflattering truths,
a contempt for reality, a hatred of fact,
an economy *verdaderamente* hell-bent
on next quarter's gain
even if it leads to the destruction of humankind,
civilization, and most of life upon earth,
as long as the shareholders get theirs,
and I get mine! I don't care! I'll be dead,
with my assault rifles lining my coffin!
Mira un narcisismo de verdugos!

"And not America alone:
the culture has spread like a bacillus
por todo el mundo
so no one can imagine an escape.
We are locked inside a rocket, and we will ride it
until it explodes against its target: we
are a nation of winners!
We must win
even in the race to suicide.
We have made our fate? *Entonces*—we deserve it."

"You speak of the game as if it's over. But what if it isn't?
What if we are midway through only? What
if we are at the beginning merely? Maybe
we are steeped in evil like a cheap teabag,
are unable to love anything but ourselves,
cannot love even ourselves without hating,
and there is no truth in us without a companion lie,
and the impossible thing is to face ourselves
without pity or rancor.
But what if it is possible,
and when we dissect our bitter heart,
the human dazzles with angels
we had no right to hope for. . . . I have names . . . "

"I know the names. I don't deny them. Even
as history's pages are blackly bloody with crimes
of evil men, the margins are often
mágicamente ilustrado: las horas muy ricas
of many a bloody chronicle
displays an art of such *delicadeza*, such gentleness,

such *sensibilidad*, like soft music
tender as a kiss, and a warm *poesía*
that makes one love the creature that could
dream up such beauty—*la belleza*,
which is nothing but *el amor encarnado*—
how do you say?—the embodiment of love.
How can one not love a creature so able
to love?"

              The moon has risen, and as it rose,
seemed to shrink, as if squeezed
into a bubble of white light
that might any moment break and vanish
splintering into ashes among brittle stars
across a sovereign darkness.

"But the newspapers are not littered with prodigies of
     love—
not even the screens of our chosen addictions
or the next sensation to leap, fully armed, from the brain,
collective or garage-bound, of Silicon Valley.
What drives us, drives us, is evil's fascination,
in love, in hate, in crime, in war:
these flatter us—only power,
only sovereign power, could leave behind so much wreckage,
The thing we fear still more than meaninglessness
is impotence. We fear
the hand we cannot raise into a fist
and crush, if we wanted; when we don't, we pretend
it is the '*in hoc signo vinces*'
of our sovereignty. But even we are not fooled.
Every so often we must prove, if we want.
Prove what? And to whom?

To ourselves. That we can destroy a foe of our will.
Every so often? *Cómo!* Every day.
So we lap up stories of manmade horrors
with a double satisfaction—in how they prove
the availability of our power—while giving a thrill
of righteous condemnation, from our moral height,
of an evil we disdainfully, sovereignly refuse.
A clever trick for a clever monkey
with too much brain; a trick to use to hide
the truths that buttress and buffet his life
even from himself. Even as the monkey chides!"

"What drives us on is love and fear,
like bees in a swarm,"
the voice within me says, speaking aloud,
both me and not me:
"more love than fear, or you've forgotten:
love of life itself, its darkness and brilliance,
touch, flavor, smell, color,
sound: the flick of a breeze, the green
of grass, the hues and tints of wild blossoming,
the microtones of light that each moment
sweep across our eyes, the fragrance
of language—if you have not smelled language,
you have not breathed at all—it intoxicates the mouth,
the ear, the mind, the teasing licks of music
that make your being quiver,
the taut trembling that is the body
in pleasure, thrown at all times, even in pain,
the exaltation of the mind in seizing at
discovery,
sensation, angle, assent, dissent, the dry

stimulus, the moist indulgence, the tart burst
on the palate, the bitter edge that makes the spine tingle
with thrill, the dream of happiness
at the heart of love's fantasy, the pool of bliss
we live at the bottom of
without knowing until it is suddenly drained,
and then our happiness is all nostalgia—we own
the uncanny ability to take the worst
of circumstance and make of it a thing
of beauty, truth, goodness that is a glory,
human genius, human victory,
refusal to be cowed by history, nature,
disease, death, madness, fate—we will defy, *I* will defy
all odds and snatch from brute fact
life, life, we will build the city
of happiness, chanting our gratitude for a world
that spun us out of light, dust, time,
and faith our ignorance hides from us, a wisdom
we never see exactly but that we
are held by, like a child in its arms.
We need fear nothing, for there is nothing to fear.

"Death? Death is nothing. We belong
to the cosmos, not ourselves,"
the voice speaks on, seems drunk, seems
almost to sing. "The cosmos
is forever, is infinite. We have no words,
no mathematics equal to it.
Understand it? Good luck!
Have faith in it. It made, formed you. Its core,
its marrow, cannot be lost;

however far you try to toss it away."

                                  A cloud
eats the moon, and the air grows black as ink,
the sky an octopus. The old man's whites
vanish, and the tide, risen, weaves the cries
of crashing waves like the wails of sinners punished
in the hell of their salvationlessness.

"There is no *cosmos*, there is *nada mayor de lo que somos*,
there are only the shadows of the cave."
The old man's voice almost disappears into the waves.
I strain to listen. "We live in a shell
that floats like a bubble among *fatuidades*,
curtains of darkness
pretending they are light,
a light revealing nothing, that can
reveal nothing except our illusions
and how deep is our solitude.
A bizarre aberration
is life in a universe otherwise
el antagonista absoluto a la vida: cosmology
is an unending slap in the face of hope.
We cannot even find life's possibility,
let alone a piece of it—say, just a planet
unas bacterias, an asteroid *de baba de estanque*, what do
    you call, "pond slime";
a world of insects only, fungus, rats—
but not anything, as Euclid sweeps the sky,
like Hubble *cojeando*—no: hobbling Hubble!—before it,
weighing *exoplanetas* on hope's duplicitous scales.
The universe is *más grande, más asombrosa*,

más hermoso, más sublime
than was ever dreamed in the stale dreams of the poets—
la poesía (what childishness is hidden in those sweet
    sounds!
La imaginación is a weak phantom compared to *la
    realidad*).
The universe not even one, but multiple!
Does nature ever create the unique, the never seen before
    or ever again?
No! She makes only families,
in molds that form individuals!
Families of existence! *Sí!* And therefore:
El universo no es un universo!
But only one of many, *un infinito*—
uno de millones of bubbles on a sea
without beginning or end, forever.
The only true poets of our time are the astronomers!
But *el multiverso* is not especially kind
or altogether welcoming to life—even though she
(cruel and generous as a woman!)
even though she invented it!
She is like an intoxicated genius, full of brilliance,
marijuana, whisky and crack cocaine,
throwing off creations *a la derecha, a la izquierda,*
and not caring where her numberless seeds fall
or where her children are orphaned:
she is too busy creating
to give two damns about protecting:
let the curators and the archivists worry about *that*!
A child today has more power at his fingertips
than Apollo, a teenager can rival Zeus

212

in havoc, a nation can wipe life from the face of the earth
like Yahweh in his prime.
La ciencia, la tecnología
have given us a scrap of knowledge, wealth
and power—*el conocimiento, la riqueza, y el poder!*—
that no one before us has ever conceived,
not for kings, not even gods—*nosotros somos los dioses!*
Yet every extension of our power
laughs at us, scorns and mocks us, since all it shows
is, *irónicamente*, how weak we are, *cómo, al final, somos
impotentes*:
subject to the limits of time, energy, matter,
a brief *espiga* of a kind of *energía
cristalizada* embracing its own extinction
in its flame. We have, *cómo se dice, borró*—erased
la trascendencia—transcendence;
we have assassinated *la Gran Esperanza*
for the sake of *pequeñas pequeñas esperanzas*
that lead to *nada*. A terrible price.
Doctor Faust, you have paid for your conquests!
Your world is *una montaña poderosa*, taller than Everest,
of *victorias pírricas*."

        The old man pauses, shaking his head
in delicate disgust.

        "Outside our little bubble of a blue planet
and its elegant technology, how long does it take
for a living being to perish?
En un minuto, si tiene suerte.
En dos minutos, si no tiene suerte!
The antagonism of the stars
is woven into our blood, our bones

are crystals of it, our thoughts fractures of its dust.
No: there is little glory in being human, *mi hermano*—
our gifts of skill, insight, invention
merely reveal the hopelessness of our case
in exquisite and eloquent detail.
Each day—each hour—bears proof
of our inanity and the emptinesss.
of the enormous stage we act on.
The evidence is overwhelming, as the lawyers say
in their eloquent closing statement: you have no choice,
ladies and gentlemen of the jury, but to convict!"

The old man grins like a wrinkled Puck
or a moonwashed skull.
The moon hangs straight overhead, small,
like a dirty street light.

                      "That is the world's mistake,
and is ours as well, but only in so far
as it *is* a mistake," the voice inside me responds,
shouting (or so it sounds to me), against this empty storm
of words. "You seem to hate science, you despise
technology, and maybe we, maybe I,
have placed too much faith in them,
was too impressed, forgot the glass pedestals they stand on,
brittle, easily seen through:
they cannot even justify themselves! They dazzle,
flatter, blind, deafen us—but we, each of us, *I*
decide how much
I give them. When they tell me I have no soul,
no self, but only a parade of delusions

of continuity over time, this *delusion* reminds them
who is master. Humanity created them;
this delusion is of humanity; it can destroy them.
I, master of the plug and the switch,
command them.
Science the truth? You make me laugh.
Science knows nothing—all it does
is push back further the horizon of our ignorance
with inspired guesses it can never prove.
Yet he is my servant
and brilliantly performs in his sphere;
though the moment he betrays me,
I stick him in his place, like any irritated god:
kindly, for he can't help being a bit of an '*idiot
savant*'; but incontrovertibly.
Sometimes his discoveries are painful but needed,
such as the ridiculous design of the human brain,
the intelligent cortex jerrybuilt on top of a monumentally
    blockheaded
cerebrum on an overexcited reptilian brain stem which
can barely wait to wreak havoc, kill its neighbor and mate
with the nearest bit of skin,
to say nothing of the atrociously worked out developmental
    scheme
of the human male...."

                        "You are beginning
to sound like me!" the old man laughs. "But, *por favor*,
do go on. *Perdóname por mi interrupción*."

"Only the better to defeat you, *viejo*.

215

Sometimes it illumines necessary facts
we need to learn—better still, facts so beautiful
it opens our sense of the immensity,
the boundless variety that is reality;
and then it is a savior we need not crucify
to deliver us from evil.
But sometimes it only wrecks my dignity and hope
for the sake of its pride—
or rather the pride of scientists—in the endless
obsessive juggling for status, dominance, power,
brief as they are and illusory as puffs of smoke.
But as soon as we recall that we invented them,
that they are subject
to our will—science, technology, scientists, geeks!—
their power evaporates like so many nightmares at dawn.
And this is true for *all* the human world:
it has no power over us we do not give it—
that *I* do not give it—and it is subject
at every moment to my power's withdrawal."

"We are lost *with* them!" The old man
is cackling wildly. "Why do you think we are flying
toward annihilation, hurtling toward
the world's ending and the human Armageddon:
ecological catastrophe on all fronts,
smothering the world in a cloud
of chemicals that exist nowhere else
en todo el universo, invented to make life
more convenient for our sweet selves,
or to kill all those creatures huddling
between us and our domination of the earth,

or even so much as a whim
('Mosquitoes? Oh my! What a nuisance? Kill them all!')
and the apocalypse of species and the coming of artificial
    intelligence
that is likely to find us (oh poetic justice!) equally irritating
('Humans? Oh my! What a nuisance! Kill them all!')
and then there is always the possibility of nuclear war *en
    cualquier momento*
(how boringly last century! But it could still kill everyone!)
The clock is ticking,
and it is almost midnight! *La ciencia?*
La tecnología? You think that you control them?
Please excuse me while I die laughing! ... "

"Then die and be quick about it. When I find myself
at loggerheads with my fellow humans,"
says the voice within,
"and they assert a power—like these!—that I deny,
I escape into the world:
my chain of consequence, immediate to transcendence,
holds me beyond defeat or death,
against, if need be, the world. And it often
'needs be' indeed!
For much of if not all the world's evils you dwell on
lie in the human will to conquer
anything but itself; command
where it was meant to serve and save,
triumph
where it was meant to bind in kindness,
to dominate where domination is a mirage
and every mountain is made of nothing more

than mist and wind.
The only human triumph, lone victory
for us, for me, is in the breath of a thought:
knowing where the diamonds of being shimmer,
where to whisper into the ear of the god
whose name is one behind the wall of night
and the eternal chaos of things.
I hand my faith to it
like a ball of twine in a labyrinth,
whose end is in my heart.
When I do thus, my heart and it so join;
the only friend I know,
though it sound insolent to say so. . . .
But that is the way to treat your god.
You will, naturally, not wish to offend
or grieve or wound the one you love,
who so loves you . . . "

The moon has long gone from the night;
behind a cloud, down the sky, past the horizon.
Nothing now spreads across the sky
like a dust rag, wiping the stars away like crumbs.
The white noise of the waves roars monotonously on.
"Your idea is beautifully mystical, my young friend,"
the old man's patient voice comes out of the deep blackness.
"I envy you your faith in one
where all I see is *el caos de las cosas y del tiempo*—
the chaos of things and time. I feel, I admit,
what little order there seems to be is the illusion
and chaos and emptiness are the final reality of all;
not order, mind, love, not even hate;

just blind energy and violence tossing
back and forth between each other and boredom,
like an infinite barracks in a post for reserves in a perpetual
    war.
We need fairy tales to cheer us, or drugs
of other kinds, from cabernet to *canabis, mezcal* to ecstasy,
ambition for wealth, fame—art, status, power. There is
nothing to meet the deepest of our *necesidades humanas:*
para la vida, la juventud y el amor forever!
We are perhaps the only living thing
that has desires that cannot be met:
we spend our lives seeking a food that does not exist—
and so we pursue *sustitutos*
irremediablemente inadecuados
and mocking!
A paradox!
But we are the paradoxical animal,
and turn on Ixion's wheel in our torments
till we pass out in a delicious dream of escaping,
waking up only to discover that escape was a cruel illusion,
and we are still fastened to the rolling wheel.
It is the most terrible fate of all, to be born a human being."

"Why have you lived so long?" the voice in me asks
the voice in the darkness. "If human life is so terrible,
why do you live? As the stoics said,
each has a quick escape, with a little, brief courage."

The darkness sighs and seems almost to smile.
"Touché, my young and clever friend!
You are right! If I find existence

so dreadful and pointless, why not end it—
my own, at least—and put me out, like a broken horse,
of my misery? It would be, at least, more honest,
and take but a small moment of bravery.
I do not have a good answer for you.
Inertia? Habit? Cowardice? or that little hope ...
ese pequeño fragmento de esperanza—I have not
yet flushed from my system,
the hope that someone—who knows! maybe you!—will
    prove me
wrong. My *espíritus animales* are incorrigible optimists,
they only believe what they want to believe
however I try to reason with them. They are convinced that,
in the end, they will—*cómo se dice?*—'disprove the
    numbers?'
disprove the numbers—
the numbers that never lie! *Ay de mí!*
They are like the man falling from the airplane who believes
that something will catch him—that something *must* catch
    him—
a flock of condors! an off-course hang glider! the last MAX
    787!
a flight of angels from paradise!—
before he hits the ground.
Hard as I try, I can't argue myself into inexistence
despite all the cunning gambits of *la razón*
and the logic that leads inexorably to the only
possible conclusion.
I feel ridiculous because I am ridiculous:
a nihilist, it would seem, who still wishes to live.
Por favor ... por favor ..." I think I hear him kneel

down on the sand.
"*Por favor:* prove me wrong, so I will feel less absurd."

The irony in his voice is like a plea;
in the invisible smile I see tears,
beneath the arrogance, the intellectual pride
an angry child crying in the night,
a child I had known, for I had been
that child, left on my own in silence,
alone in the dark and dreaming of a love
withdrawn into ice forever.

The voice within me nevertheless responded.
"I cannot prove anything, I do not know anything.
What I have is doubt at war with trust
that, however terrible the future is—
the humanly wrought and administered hell
we re-create with each new generation—
the madness of our dance of wealth and death,
our feverish vulgarity and chronic bad faith,
the shabbiness and disgust of daily life,
the greed and cowardice and self-deception
(beside which mere falsehoods are almost quaint)
that paralyze us as we destroy
the life that we know, the life we have known,
the life we believed was possible,
and prepare our annihilation
with the lunatic conscientiousness of an army corps of
    demons—
to say nothing of the insults of disease and age,
the cruelty of the diseased mind, the self-defeating brutality

of insolent crime and proud war—
despite all these—even, in some way
because of them—the evils they define
define this good:
to conquer them,
to make
out of this mud, these stones,
out of the wrath of these seas,

joy,

kindness,

delight,

a common love and common joy,
profoundest satisfaction in each other and ourselves,

a meaning and purpose for life:

out of the cold of infinite space crossing the violence of
    infinite time,
a home for joy and love.

For we are clever monkeys.
Can we deepen cleverness into wisdom,
learn the shifting balance
of freedom and love, reverence and liberty
(none can bear life without safety,
though safety grow a cage;
no breath's worth drawing without freedom,

though freedom be a danger to all;
of one too much is a prison,
of the other too much is a hell),
and make of the blue globe a manor
inside which lives a home
for life in its darkling splendor,
bright birth and the payment of death
for the infinite debt of being?
And crush and mold cold despair
into grist for creation's mills?

"Build, make, form, mold
in worlds in unending creation,
sing so softly you only can hear,
let your heart dance
in the mouth of the lion. For the creator
of this, of us, though hidden
from us as the lion is hidden
from its fleas, the wilderness from its wolves—
though everything we see is nothing
but, of it, an emanation
is in love with its creation
no less than the dancer
is in love with her own dancing—
loving, critical, demanding more:
truer delicacy, braver truth,
deeper beauty—sometimes turning
the whole creation inside out
from a monstrous curiosity—
but in love forever with the dance—
like that paradigm of inspired impracticality,

a poet, idealist who sacrifices his hours
inventing a few pearled strings of words
that meet his highly personal terms
of the true and the beautiful and the good,
though yielding small fame,
precious little wealth, and no power,
for him or his posterity—
just a fleeting breath
of a serene affirmation
lost a breath later,
and a strange pride that keeps his head high
though humankind else shrugs, puzzled,
suspicious, and disdainful. (Especially other poets!)

"The world is such a poet, such a dancer,
obsessive creator spinning patterns from clouds.
All that is, will be, has been,
will have been beyond the end of time.
We have, I have, *now*.
That may be the only immortality.
My work is at the end of the world's hands.

"Like earth, coal into diamond, we
hold, squeeze, fire darkness into light.
In my mind I hold the universe
like a jewel in my hand,
comprehend it, and myself within it,
from immense grandeur
to tiniest refinement, host
the tent of the circus of being—
for do not forget, phantom of despair:

in her wild gentleness,
delicacy, power,
to infinity, through eternity, she lives.

"Thus I, thus you,
despite the masking miserliness
of slippery time and granite space,
my destiny to decay and death, your
compulsive follies, my grotesqueness,
your unfathomable evil, the
appearance we proffer to the stars'
dead laughter, of being so much
illegitimate progeny of mud and the divine—
I, beaten, broken, by hate, by fear, injustice, death,
was, am, shall be,
a god's—however he disowns me—
child."

The darkness was at its deepest. The voice within me
sounded strange, hollow, as though
alone in an empty room.
I waited for the old man
to answer, but all I heard was waves,
suddenly distant, as though withdrawing with the tide.
Then I saw a dim glow above the horizon
and watched as it grew stronger, felt my shadow
deepen with the appearance of the light.
The sky grew dull and stretched with cloud ribbons
and flattened out. The sea looked like pewter.
Then an edge of startling brightness
appeared under the scrambled glow,

and the sun edged upward, red, golden.

I turned to look at the old man,
but there was no one there. I was alone on the beach.
Had he walked away in disgust at my last speech?
Had he given up on someone so incorrigibly naive?
Had he even been there at all? No, he'd been there,
of that I was sure. Perhaps he had thrown himself
back into the sea from which he had come.
I watched as the sun rose like a head or like an eye
staring across a world that was all sky,
and I felt myself drowning in sky and light.

And a form broke from the sun and the far
calling of the waves. Nebulous as fog or cloud,
it seemed to step toward me over sand
brilliant and slippery as glass,
and I saw behind it a throng
of brilliant, smiling—were they angels?—
misty and fragrant as the breeze
that lifted from the ocean.
The glowing form seemed to speak,
and it was the voice inside me,
bright and soft as an angel's,
or as I would imagine an angel's.

"Know this," it spoke, as if close to my ear,
almost a whisper, and I strained to hear.

"Know this: we are perpetual
creation, an infinite world.

We enter time to work out
endless possibilities.
Know this: your purpose here
is to work out possibility.
Know this: we are nature,
nature is ourselves.
You are our hands and eyes
as we are your eyes and hands.
The power of infinite evil and good
is in your eyes and hands.
The ultimately beautiful is the ultimately real.
Know this. You are free. So: choose."

And the smile of the nebulously glowing figure
was so intense, it almost burned my face.

And suddenly the throng of angels,
and the sea and the shore and the sky
rang, like all the bells in all the cities
were ringing across the earth—
though how could that be? How could any of this be?
And I was surrounded by the flocking and singing of many
    birds.
And the waves glittered before me,
and I heard laughter, friendly and welcoming.
And the air smelled of shells and brine and roses
and smoke and perfume and wine and apples and brandy.
And a crab made mock with a clam, and a blade of grass
traced the outline of the loveliest of girls in the dunes
to the dip of a breeze and a turn of a sun ray. And a falcon
traded mysteries with a dove. And wind

swept up the sand in a glory of wind devils
swirling in shapes of Carmen, Marilyn, Venus,
created in a moment, in a moment cast back
to sand and wind. And clouds whitened into foam
and winds and galleons moving over the azure like a sea,
a moment anticipated, here, lost, once, forever.

And the sun as it rose opened and filled the sea morning sky:
infinite, eternal, flashing, fugitive, fleeting, dying, bright.

Miracle

Don't believe in miracles. Depend on them.
— Laurence J. Peter

The Night of the Star

They'd been traveling all day, since before sunrise,
and now it was dark and snowing.
Then the car broke down, and now this cracker . . .
"You just got bad timing," the burly man had told them.
"Nobody round here got any rooms tonight, sorry."
That was the last straw. "Damn all,
it's Christmas Eve, man!" . . . "It's all right, Jay."
The girl, her little heart pounding,
looked the motel owner, unflinching, in the eye.

Sheesh, thought the man. How old are these kids?
Him, skinny, rasta hair, bitter eyes, eighteen maybe,
her, tiny, cornrows, more in control than her dude,
sixteen—less!
And what are they doing in Red Bluff?
The nearest ghetto's in Oakland . . .
Oh no . . . there's the problem. The small swollen body,
the perfect little sphere at her tummy
peeking through a tatty coat. . . .

"Well," he said, with some reluctance,
"we aren't s'pposed to do this,
but there's a corner in the garage we sometimes rent out.
It's not legal, so we have to charge more . . . " "More?"
sputtered the angry boy. "For a garage?
We gotta sleep on cement?" "Now hold your horses, there's a
  cot—"
"A cot?!" "Actually, two cots, and blankets, and a table, and a utility
  sink,

231

and a ceiling light. You allergic to dogs or cats?
We keep Rex and Tina down there."
The lobby windows shook in the wind.
Jay gave him the knife eye. This was no good.
He'd promised he'd take care of her when they got out,
they couldn't stay in Tracy, with her parents there,
but why was doing the right thing so damn hard?
Why was he blocked everywhere he turned?
He felt humiliated as he looked at the girl.
"You OK with this, Myra?" he mumbled.
She nodded. "OK," he said, "we'll take it," after cursing
silently the motel, the owner, Red Bluff and the weather.
Myra had been holding her breath, and let out a sigh.

An hour later the two young people were settled
in a freezing corner of concrete and dirty pipes,
half hidden behind an SUV
under a hanging bulb. A colorless mutt had growled
when they came in, then seemed to give them a pass.
A mangy calico cat was fast asleep in its basket near a litter box.
"If we weren't black," said Jay, getting madder by the moment,
"he'd've at least let us sleep in the lobby,
the old white fucker!" "Jay, don't," said Myra.
"Don't use such language around the baby."
Jay looked at her like she was crazy.
"It's not even born yet! What's it gonna care what anybody says?"
"How do you know? You inside me listening?
Anyway, we all got a roof over our heads for the night."
She heard the wind roaring the snow down from distant Shasta.
"Be thankful, Jay." "I'll be damned first!"
He pulled a cot away from the freezing wall,

and Myra lay down and curled up around her tummy,
stroking it and humming a lullaby.
They lay side by side on the cots, tucked up in blankets
and listening to the wind and snow roaming like a hungry animal
      outside,
covering the land with an icy whiteness
under a starless sky.

Finally almost asleep, Jay got up to turn off the light.
He heard something from his lady;
she was no longer humming, and her hand on her tummy was still.
It had just passed midnight.
"Merry Christmas, baby," said Jay, and he kissed her on the forehead.
There was a look of intense concentration in her eyes.
"Hey, baby ... you all right?" She turned to him and tried to pull
      herself up.
"Jay ..." Her look of concentration deepened. "Jay ... Jay? ...
I think ... I think it ..." Suddenly she looked scared. "Jay—I think
      it's ... "
... Holy shit holy shit holy shit not here not now ... !

A clutch of teens were passing a joint behind Sal's.
"Hey man, this stuff so strong, I can see Santa Claus comin'
over Redding," one was giggling. "That's no Santa,
that's a drone, bitch, and he is coming after yo' tight ass!"
Suddenly someone they didn't know walked out of the darkness.
He wore a dark raincoat, which didn't make much sense;
it wasn't raining, after all; the snow had lightened,
and a few flakes whirled giddily in the street light.
The boys stopped and stared. "A narc," one whispered,
killing the joint with his boot.

"Or some tranny freak," another sneered.
It had the figure of a man but a woman's face,
it spoke softly but locked their eyes with its own:
each thought the figure looked at him alone.
"None of the above." It smiled. "Sorry to disappoint." The boys
were suddenly frightened. "Don't be afraid.
Across the alley there's something you ought to see.
I promise you won't regret it." It pointed to a garage
where a light was burning.
"Hey, it's late, man. And it's Christmas, I gotta get home."
"Wait. Just go. And look." It gazed at them expectantly.
"What have you got to lose? It's good news." And it smiled
again that smile they found so intimidating.
"Good news for all of us." Then it seemed to disappear. "Peace . . ."

"Man, that stuff is strong," said one of the boys, flipping away his
    toke.
"Was that hippie-dippie or what?" another joked, nervously.
"So gay!" another scoffed.

But they went to the garage anyway. A young black man and
    woman—
really a boy and girl, much the same age they were,
but looking worn out, wary and anxious—
looked up as they came in, from a tiny black baby
wrapped up in a towel and blanket
and lying half in a sink. From a hole near the ceiling
came a sound of pigeons, their sleepy
heads looking out. A mongrel dog
crouched nearby, its head cocked quizzically,
an ageing calico cat sat on a rickety tea table,

its eyes probing and intent;
they all stared at the infant,
who lay watching them curiously,
in the unfocused way babies have;
seeming to be wondering where on earth he was.
He burbled something and his eyes were bright.
He was black as night, and he shone.
The boys, still high, fell to their knees.

Sometime later, there was a tap at the utility door,
and three old men came in, one with a raggedy beard,
one with a funny hat, the third with his fingers
covered with beer-can rings. Their clothing,
dirty and torn, was thick with snow,
and they stood for a moment shaking it off inside the door
like a trio of sheepdogs just let in from the winter cold.
Then they saw the baby with its mother,
and they stopped and stared with a look of wild joy.

 "I tol' you I be right," said the one with the hat. "He da man!
He come back at last! Just like he promise!" "How k'n you tell?"
The first just smiled and shrugged, as if marveling at his own
        wisdom.
They all seemed slightly inebriated.
The ringed man made an intricate, unsteady bow.
"I hope you'll 'scuse us, ma'am,
we come all the way from way over," motioning vaguely east,
"through a nasty night, just to get here. And we a little . . . wuss for
        wear . . ."
Myra smiled, exhausted from the long day and the labor
and the birth, and not at all sure just what was going on.

The man, with excruciating care, removed his rings
and placed them, one at a time, near the baby, their brightness
glimmering like his eyes. The two other men
also placed small offerings: a vial of cheap perfume,
a little aromatic stone, and a handful of costume jewelry.
"Why are you giving us these things?" the girl asked.
"You really don' know?"
The man in the hat looked genuinely surprised.
"Well, it ain't for me to say..." "It all we got to give,"
the man with the raggedy beard said bashfully. And the three
homeless men sat down on the cement, near the boys,
who had been watching, half way between cracking up
and a weird feeling of awe.

"What are they all doin' here, what are they all talkin' about?"
Jay, upset and offended, muttered to himself.
Were they making fun of them? Who did they think they were?
Did they think this "little black baby Jesus" bullshit was some kind
    of joke?
If it was, it was a sick joke by a bunch of white motherfuckers,
and he would take all of them out! "Shh," said Myra,
and she shook her head wearily at her man,
then took her newborn baby
who was at last starting to cry, and opening up her blouse,
her eyes shiny with wonder at this new, astonishing creation,
let him greedily feed.

Jay turned his back on the whole weird scene and went outside—
man, he needed some air. This was too motherfuckin' crazy!
Man, this was fucked up!
He had never felt so mad, ashamed and disgusted.

He started crying. Why was this happening to them?
He wasn't even sure it was his kid!

The snow had stopped, the sky was deep, empty and clear.
He looked up, the tears streaming down his face,
and his jaw dropped open.
He saw something he had never seen before in his life:
filling half the night sky, hanging straight above him,
was a great, brilliant star.

The Socialist's Garden of Verses

is not of poems made
alone. In man and woman
are hearts of earth and water
where roots of roses tangle
with the serene potato,
the skins of peach and apple
and the plump red sweet tomato,
the fruits of earth from which all
humanity is made:
faith and hope and charity,
and love of truth and kindness,
belief in good and beauty:
these are the pleasing verses
from which is made the garden
of hope you will engender
after you have closed
this book and put it away.

The dragonfly awaits you,
the beetle, ant and butterfly,
the sun is high over the garden,
the fragrant grasses call you.
Our work is just beginning,
the earth and sky are waiting.
Take my singing with you
out into the day.

Notes and Acknowledgements

"The Genesis of T#$%/landia" is adapted from the opening chapter of Genesis, the King James Version of the Bible.

"Invocation" is adapted from the opening lines of George Chapman's translation of Homer's *Iliad* ("Ilias" in Chapman's version).

"T#$%! Chaucer" is adapted from the Prologue to Geoffrey Chaucer's *Canterbury Tales.*

"The Love Song of Donald J.T#$%!" is adapted from "The Love Song of J.Alfred Prufrock," by T. S. Eliot.

"Mr.T#$%/ollinax" is adapted from "Mr.Apollinax," by T. S. Eliot.

"T#$%! Among the Nightingales" is adapted from "Sweeney Among the Nightingales," by T. S. Eliot.

"T#$%! Emily" is adapted from "The Soul selects its own Society," by Emily Dickinson.

"Basho T#$%!"is adapted from the haiku of Matsuo Basho.

"The Waste T#$%!" is adapted from "The Waste Land," by T. S. Eliot.

The poems in "Faust Closes the Books on the Modern Age" appeared first in *Caveat Lector.* The poems in "Prelude in Hell," several poems in "Dispatches From Pandemia," and an early version of "The Night of the Star," differently titled, originally appeared in *Synchronized Chaos International Magazine.* Early versions of a number of other poems originally appeared as postings in Facebook.

Special thanks to Steven Hill and Richelle Slota for their helpful suggestions regarding a number of poems in this collection, but especially "Señor Despair and the Angel." And thanks above all to Peter Bush for kindly correcting my Spanish in that poem.

Christopher Bernard's books include the poetry collections *Chien Lunatique* and *The Rose Shipwreck: Poems and Photographs*, the short-fiction collections *Dangerous Stories for Boys* and *In the American Night*, and the novels *A Spy in the Ruins*, *Voyage to a Phantom City*, and *Meditations on Love and Catastrophe at The Liars' Cafe*. He is founder and co-editor of the webzine *Caveat Lector*. He lives in San Francisco.

CPSIA information can be obtained
at www.ICGtesting.com
Printed in the USA
FSHW012133210221
78819FS